Copyright 2026. Wanderlust
Publishing, a Div of SFS Inc.
All Rights Reserved

A Note from the Author

Hi there. I'm Miist. My goal as a singer-songwriter is to be part of something bigger and better. I hope that in the pages of this book you'll find a place of refuge where you feel safe to laugh, smile, listen to great music and learn. Let's take a break from the craziness of our lives to discover simple, forgotten ways to change your world in only fifteen seconds a day. In doing so, we can remind each other of what it means to be human.

I never want you to feel overwhelmed by being asked to do things you cannot do. We are all imperfect and have our issues and challenges. Always do what you can to the best of your ability while remembering it's not a game of comparison or competition. The ideas we discuss are about changing the way we live our lives, and they should always be positive and fun. Sometimes it's hard if we've been out of the habit, but it's worthwhile when we put in the effort. The only failure is giving up. Please don't give up.

I should add that I love that you are here reading this book. However, I am not a mental health professional, nor a doctor. I'm someone just like you who struggles, learns, and grows.

Please do not take this book as a substitute for seeking professional help. If you are having dark thoughts right now that you can't control, please reach out to 911 or 988, the suicide prevention line.

As of this writing, The Smile Project—which led to the Make Me Smile with Miist podcast—has been adapted into sixteen language editions and involves dozens of artists and musicians from around the world. You can learn more about the song on my website, miistthesinger.com/smile.

You can find me on Instagram and Facebook as MiisttheSinger. I look forward to reading your comments, messages, and feedback regarding this book. My music is available on YouTube or any other streaming platform under Miist or MiistTheSinger. Let's build a family and a vision of the future that looks happier, more fulfilling, and more meaningful. Let's learn to smile again.

This is "Make Me Smile."

Table of Contents

Could You Lend Me a Smile

One day, as I was walking in a park with my family, the thought came to mind: We have forgotten what it means to be human. I noticed no one looked at each other. No one smiled.

When I say we've forgotten what it means to be human, I mean we have forgotten that we're truly a special creation. We weren't made only to live but to enjoy life. The things that bring us the greatest joys are not what we take, but what we freely give: a hug, a hand to hold, a voice to comfort, a word to encourage, or even just a smile. We can find joy in simply being a friend and giving strength to someone in need.

One of those small joys is a smile. Smiles are hardwired into our amazing psyche to provide endorphins, both when we smile and when someone smiles at us. Our natural and reflexive response to a smile is to return the smile. The positive feelings that smiling causes can carry us through some really difficult times.

Not smiling back at someone is a conscious decision, making us literally fight our muscles' natural inclination to smile back. In our world today, we have essentially trained ourselves *not* to do something that is part of human nature. That's pretty messed up when you think about it.

A smile is one of the most powerful and valuable gifts we can give, as humans, but we have forgotten how to give and freely accept them. We hoard them for only the most special occasions, almost like we have a finite number to give. We divvy them out like a reserved wine to only our closest friends and family. Can you imagine what a difference it would make for our neighbors, cities, and families if we would give smiles indiscriminately and generously instead?

What if everyone around the world started smiling at each other constantly? Do you think there would be fewer fights, arguments, and angry words? The answer, obviously, is yes. Those who disagree, I would venture to say, certainly do not smile enough.

I began thinking about how a simple smile might touch so many lonely people after reading an article that told the story of a young man in Tokyo. This man was found deceased in his apartment, having died alone. He had been there for weeks. In Japan, as in other countries, this has become so common that it's become known as "lonely death."

I will never forget his story. Even now, I imagine him walking down the streets, the sounds of thousands of footsteps passing by, and I wonder if anyone will bother to lend him a smile.

I see him walking on those crazy, busy streets of Tokyo, amidst the sounds of cars and buses, smells wafting from restaurants, and the vivid colors of neon signs. Millions of people pass by him.

I feel his pain as he glances at people's faces, hoping to see a glimpse of kindness or a smile. As my mind follows him, I imagine one or two people making eye contact, sparking a flicker of hope inside him.

Envisioning more and more people walking by, I yearn to see that swelling of support that will save his life.

This story inspired me to write a song called "Could You Lend Me a Smile." In the song, I express my hope, using the sound of the cellos and violins.

In my song, I imagine people's attitudes changing and throngs of people coming to his aid—not just to his aid individually, but for all of us. They rise up to change the way we live our day-to-day lives and to connect in the most basic of human responses—a smile.

I included background voices in the song, starting in the second verse, to represent the whispers of the throngs of people. Their voices are so faint you aren't sure if they're real or imagined. Hearing them has to be intentional.

The man feels this, as well. He is daring to hope but isn't sure if it's just in his imagination.

I imagine that man's life could have had a different outcome if only a few people showed him kindness, fighting against the inclination to isolate and withdraw, and instead risking a smile. If he had received that most basic of support, he just might have lived. So, I asked myself if I was willing to be one of those people.

"Could You Lend Me A Smile"

Before you continue reading, I invite you to experience the song "Could You Lend Me A Smile." You can scan the QR code below to see the English music video of this song. The song had so much global support that it ended up being released in sixteen language versions. You can find all of them on my YouTube channel, MiistTheSinger, or on any streaming platform. Listen carefully to hear the elements of hope in the strings and the whispering of crowds in the background.

I wanted to write the piano to represent the footsteps of people walking around the man. The piano parts are played by the GRAMMY®-nominated and renowned pianist, Philip Krohnengold.

The cello was critical to the English version of the song, so I asked to be introduced to Adele's cellist, the brilliant and GRAMMY®-winning artist, Eru Matsumoto. I heard about what she was doing and the projects she was working on that combine science and music. These projects aim to help people in different ways, working with Harvard and Stanford to help people improve their sleep quality and depression. I felt our goals were in line with each other's and saw that Eru was also bringing hope to people. So, as I wrote the cello into the song, I didn't view the instrument as a symbol of sadness, as it usually is, used in music. After meeting Eru, the cello in this song became a sound of hope. When she starts playing, she takes the lead, bringing hope. Then you'll hear a small group of violins responding to that hope. That's why the violins are lighter in the song, compared to the cello. They are following the cello from far away.

Then I was introduced to Nathalie Bonin, an internationally acclaimed GRAMMY® violinist. She's very much loved by everyone I talk to, and she's their go-to girl for violin. This made me very curious about her, and now I totally understand why she is so loved. It was my honor to have her join me on SMILE. Her violin perfectly adds a voice of hope and love to the song.

Over a total of sixteen language versions, the individual artists and their instruments added to this story of that man's life to make it a global movement.

One of the first artists we worked with was an amazing Vietnamese artist, Dong Lan. She travels all over the world; however, her home country is Vietnam, so she doesn't have many friends in the U.S. when she visits. When we met, she was experiencing loneliness, so the song really resonated with her.

As we talked about the song, I could hear in her voice that she truly felt every word as she recorded her vocals. Her voice brought me to tears. Her singing style is very cool, combining jazz with traditional Vietnamese singing, with an incredibly expressive voice.

Scan the QR code below to hear the Vietnamese version of "Could

You Lend Me a Smile."

As we expanded to include more languages, we learned that Brazil suffered from a lot of loneliness during the COVID-19 pandemic. With this in mind, we started looking for star talent in Brazil. GRAMMY®-winning producer Emilio Miler found the amazing Bruna Black. We recorded her Brazilian Portuguese version of the song, and she brought in a completely different style.

Scan the QR code below to hear the Brazilian Portuguese version of "Could You Lend Me a Smile."

One thing I love so much about this project is how each singer brings in a different culture and style, even though we're interpreting the exact same message. It taught me that in different countries and different areas, we could all be experiencing loneliness, just in a different way.

Just as we can experience loneliness anywhere in the world, we can also be determined to help, no matter where we are. I wanted to start by finding out how people felt about smiling. This process began in Marin County, California, but during the SMILE movement's inception, I also visited Monterey, California, with my family. We walked the Monterey pier one day to interview people there.

I found it enlightening to realize how difficult it was to get people to talk to us about smiling. More than 90 percent barely acknowledged our greetings, and about 75 percent didn't even make eye contact. It just reemphasized to me how important our project is. We need to change the way we look at each other. We have lost our social graces and even common courtesy. However, in the end, we met a few very nice people.

One person we interviewed said they try to smile at people when they're out on walks because it makes them happy, even if people don't smile back. They theorized that some people are distracted by their own struggles or just unaware of their surroundings, and that might be the reason others don't smile back.

Another interviewee noted that when a community stops smiling, it shows there's not much hope left in that community.

In the wake of this realization, my family and I decided to smile at everyone during our walks—no looking down at the sidewalk or avoiding eye contact. Instead, we were determined to purposefully look at everyone we could—and smile. As we started smiling at others, we sometimes saw the same people multiple times during one walk. It became common that the second or third time we saw them, they started smiling back, even the people who had ignored our smiles initially.

It changed the way we lived. And, as with many of the most basic human actions, I'm sure it helped us as much or more than it affected others.

Fifteen Seconds to Change Your World

Our first fifteen-second tip is really simple, yet so powerful: Smile at the people you come in contact with today, on purpose. Look them in the eye and give them the beautiful gift of a smile from a stranger, brightening both their day and yours.

Count how many people you're able to smile at and take note of their reactions. How did they respond? How did it make you feel to smile at them?

You may not get a smile back, but you will still feel better. If you are at work, smile at someone next to you. If you are in a coffee shop, find another patron to smile at. If you're alone, go to a mirror and smile at yourself. Show a lot of teeth. It's OK to look goofy.

If someone—including yourself—thinks you're a little crazy, that's OK. At least they will remember that person who smiled at them, and just maybe they will smile at someone else. We're made in such a way that smiling releases endorphins. It makes us feel good. So, give it a smile.

My Fifteen Seconds

On my weekly podcast episodes, I personally participate in the weekly fifteen-second actions I ask you to do. Throughout this book, I'll be sharing a little about how I did that. Together, we can make the world better, one fifteen-second action at a time.

For this episode's fifteen-second action, I went to smile at my mom. I didn't tell her why. She definitely thought I was crazy, and that is OK.

Citations and references for this chapter are located at the end of the book.

Episodes 3

Why Gratitude?

A poem from *Harmony* by Whitney Hanson reads as follows:

They say, when you grow up in a burning house, you think the whole world is on fire.

I didn't grow up in a burning house.

I grew up in a house where we hid the flame.

I grew up in a house where everyone was secretly burning on the inside, but we didn't dare speak of it.

I grew up in a house where we wore our armor like a badge of honor and pretended that nothing ever hurt us.

For so long, I thought it was only me who felt like I was deteriorating from the inside.

Now, I put my flames on paper because I need you to know that there are others whose fires are kept inside like a scorching secret.

I will not let you burn alone.

I really like this poem because, in a way, it reflects how I feel about sharing my songs with the world. Because of the way I grew up, I always had a hard time sharing my deepest feelings with anyone. I kept them inside of me until I was thirty-four years old, when I discovered songwriting. Finally, all the feelings I had been hiding from everyone else were able to come out freely in my songs. When I share those songs with the world, it's me saying, "Look, I'm struggling with the same things as you are, and you don't have to deal with it alone."

When I first started writing songs, I found myself working through a lot of trauma. Who knew that songwriting would become such an emotional outlet and opportunity to heal? I'm very grateful to God that I was given this ability—which, admittedly, even I don't understand—as it has healed me more than I could have imagined possible.

Some of my greatest traumas are rooted in the fact that, at five years old, my parents dropped me off and essentially abandoned me at a boarding school. My father never returned, and even my mother did not come back into my life until my teenage years.

A lot of resentment built up due to that, and even though my mom supported me through my liver cancer surgery when I was twenty-seven, I found that I still harbored many negative feelings about my childhood, my father, and her.

I decided I didn't like those feelings. I wanted to heal them to help myself as well as to set a good example for my stepdaughter, who was abandoned by her mother at the same age as I had been. I knew from personal experience how negatively abandonment can impact a life, and I didn't want her to experience those same lost decades. But I knew I needed to heal my own trauma to teach her how to deal with hers. So, naturally, I wrote a song. I originally wrote it in Chinese, as that is my mother tongue. Also, I wanted my mom to hear it as she didn't (and still doesn't) speak English. Later, I released it in English, and it is one of my most personal, meaningful songs. It is called "She." This song is about gratitude, but it's more than that—it's a way to heal.

"<u>She</u>"

Before you continue reading, I invite you to experience the song "She." You can find the song on my YouTube channel (MiistTheSinger) or any streaming platform.

I didn't play the song for my mom right away. I feared she wouldn't understand it—or maybe I was still hoping for a spontaneous apology for how she had abandoned me during my childhood, even though I knew that was highly unlikely. I think I also knew that once my mom heard the song, she would think I felt good about my childhood, but that wasn't true. I have felt abandoned my whole life because of the events the song talks about. However, I shared only my gratitude in

"She," not the pain or sadness.

When I finally did let her listen to it, she thought it was "Nice." Ow. On the inside, her reaction disappointed me. I guess I was surprised that she wasn't more touched by it, especially since I had mentioned only the good, leaving out the bad. But then I reminded myself that the song wasn't meant solely for her. I had written the song mainly for myself.

I wanted to remember all the reasons I should be grateful to my mother instead of the reasons to feel negative. The negative feelings felt lousy to carry around. I felt like my life was being defined by my abandonment, which made me feel like a victim. I didn't want to think of myself like that.

There is a TEDx talk by Christina Kota, "Kiss Your Brain: The Science of Gratitude." She's a teacher and a psychologist of human nature. She is also fighting brain cancer. She explained that, to help encourage her students, she would tell them to "kiss your brain." It was only after she was diagnosed with brain cancer that, as a way of healing, she started applying that encouragement to herself. She wasn't talking about a miracle cure for cancer—she was still undergoing treatment for brain cancer. Rather, it was a way to heal the way she thought.

When she was first diagnosed, everyone encouraged her to fight. They would say, with the best intentions, "You are a fighter. You'll win the fight." She found that sentiment exhausting and didn't like the idea of fighting anything or worrying. So, she changed the way she thought. "Instead of thinking about what my body was doing wrong," she said, "I started contemplating what my body was doing right, and I found myself grateful, grateful that I had an amazing brain, thankful for science, medicine, and my medical team."

She noticed a change in her attitude toward the disease, a change from fear and hostility to one of peace. This took her full circle, back to how she had taught her students to "kiss your brain."

This wasn't just thinking positive thoughts, but living a life of gratefulness and thankfulness, a way of life that had scientifically been proven in numerous studies to increase peace, happiness, and stronger relationships, and decrease physical pain and depression. Gratefulness activates the prefrontal cortex and can restructure harmful thoughts, rewiring the brain. The more we activate it, the stronger it becomes. Even pessimists can change their brain chemistry.

I didn't realize it at the time, but I was doing this when I wrote "She." I was reminding myself to be grateful instead of resentful. After writing the song, I still remember my childhood, but it immensely helped my relationship with my mom. She didn't change, but I changed the way I felt about her. My gratitude brings me so much more peace and contentment than I had before.

Gratitude is unique because it can be done 100 percent by ourselves. It doesn't have to involve anyone else to have an amazing effect on us in just a few seconds. A Harvard study found: One group wrote about things they were grateful for that had occurred during the week. A second group wrote about daily irritations or things that had displeased them, and the third wrote about events that had affected them (without emphasis on whether they were positive or negative). After 10 weeks, those who wrote about gratitude were more optimistic and felt better about their lives. Surprisingly, they also exercised more and had fewer visits to physicians than those who focused on sources of aggravation.

The same Harvard study said, "In positive psychology research, gratitude is strongly and consistently associated with greater happiness. Gratitude helps people feel more positive emotions, relish good experiences, improve their health, deal with adversity, and build strong relationships."

Another leading researcher in this field, Dr. Martin EP Seligman, a psychologist at the University of Pennsylvania, tested the impact of various positive psychology interventions on 411 people, each compared with a control assignment. Their assignment was to write and personally deliver a letter of gratitude to someone who had never been properly thanked. Participants immediately exhibited a huge increase in happiness scores. This impact was greater than that from any other intervention, with benefits lasting for a month.

Other studies looked at how being grateful can improve relationships. For example, a study of couples found that individuals who took time to express gratitude for their partner not only felt more positive toward the other person but also felt more comfortable expressing concerns about the relationship.

Of course, expressing gratitude can be even more powerful in practice. Think of a time when you were working hard. Perhaps you were so tired and just wanted to be done with the task. Then maybe someone came along and said, "You are doing an amazing job."

What does that do to you? It provides energy and encouragement. You likely found the strength to do a bit more.

The Harvard Health article added this interesting thought: Managers who remember to say "thank you" to people who work for them may find that those employees feel motivated to work harder.

Researchers at the Wharton School at the University of Pennsylvania randomly divided university fundraisers into two groups. One group made phone calls to solicit alumni donations in the same way they always had. The second group, assigned to work on a different day, received a pep talk from the director of annual giving, who told the fundraiser participants she was grateful for their efforts. The following week, the university employees who heard her message of gratitude made 50 percent more fundraising calls than those who did not.

To apply this, you don't have to be a manager. When you see someone working hard, whether on the street, in a cafe, or sweeping the sidewalk at home, tell them, "You are doing a great job." Think about how good that could make them feel.

Another example of how gratitude benefits you comes from an article from UCLA. It says that taking a moment to be thankful can cause physiological changes in your body that activate the parasympathetic nervous system. This is the part of your nervous system that helps you rest and digest. The feelings of gratitude and the response it elicits help lower your blood pressure, heart rate, and breathing, promoting overall relaxation.

If we were all determined to be more grateful for just a few seconds each day, our world would be a better place. Don't forget to include yourself in this. If no one else is saying it, give yourself a big smile and tell yourself, "You're doing a great job today." Even if all you've done today is to show gratitude, you have done a great job as a human being. You have contributed and helped to make your world better.

In our interviews on this topic, I asked, "What do you feel grateful for?" People had a lot of things to talk about: weather, animals, or even the fact that they were alive, just to name a few.

They also said they thought being grateful was a very important thing in our everyday lives. Someone else noted how we often forget to be grateful for what we have because we are conditioned to always want more.

After these interviews, it occurred to me that some people view expressing gratitude as a weakness. But which is easier—to feel like the system is unfair, or to find a way to be grateful despite that? In a difficult world, it's hard to feel grateful. It is easy to feel like a victim.

Let me say that again. It's *hard* to feel grateful. It is easy to feel like a victim—probably because so many are.

Gratitude helps people refocus on what they have instead of what they lack. When the LA fires were going on in January of 2025, in the first three days, everyone was commenting on how angry and sad they were at what was happening. Indeed, it was a terrible tragedy. Still, in that tragedy, there were reasons to feel grateful.

How about all those first responders who put their lives on the line? How about all those neighbors looking out for one another? Great tragedies give us the opportunity for great compassion, and by showing our gratitude to those people, perhaps we give them the strength they need to keep going. Isn't that what we all need? A little push to just keep us going?

My husband likes to tell the story of a tourist on vacation to a faraway island paradise. The tourist goes down to the beach one morning and finds a fisherman coming in with his catch. The fisherman had a few fish, but not many, and the tourist asked why he had come in so early.

The fisherman replied that he had enough for the day, plus a few he could sell for some extra cash. Now that he had enough, he was going home to spend time with his family, including his young son.

The tourist asked the fisherman, "Why not just stay out a little longer so you can get more fish?"

The fisherman asked, "Why would I do that?"

"So you can make extra money," the tourist replied.

"What would I do with the money?"

"Well, if you saved enough, you could buy another boat, then you could hire more of your friends and make even more money."

The fisherman thought for a moment. "Then what would I do?"

"Well, if you worked hard for a decade or so, you could have a fleet of boats to catch so many fish that you could retire."

"And do what?" the fisherman wondered.

Without a pause, the tourist answered, "You could move to an island paradise and have lots of time to relax with your family."

The fisherman looked at him, smiled, then turned to walk away.

We are told by the system we live in to keep running on the treadmill of productivity—more education, more money, more fame. We are told those are the things that will make us happy, but we are a world full of unhappy, lonely, and anxious people.

Maybe we need to reevaluate what is really important and get back to just being human.

Fifteen Seconds to Change Your World

Think of things you are grateful for. If you're in a really bad situation right now, it might not be easy to find something to be grateful for, but do your best anyway. You could be grateful to see the sunset, a cute dog, or a neighbor who is always smiling. You can be grateful that you have food to eat or a friend you can call.

My Fifteen Seconds

I'm grateful for the air and breathing. I'm grateful for my family who loves me, for who I am, and I'm grateful for my dog, who is growing very old but still kicking. I found these thoughts made me smile, and I felt happier inside.

Citations and references for this chapter are located at the end of the book.

Episodes 4

Imagine Who You Want to Be

In the last chapter, we talked about the reason why I wrote the song "She," which is a tribute to my mother. Specifically, I wrote it for her to express gratitude for everything she did. But in reality, she and my father dropped me off at a boarding school when I was five years old, and I didn't see much of her again until my teenage years. My father never returned. Last week, I talked about why I wrote a song about gratitude instead of one about resentment: To heal myself. Feeling grateful makes us feel peace, contentment, and happiness, whereas resentment... well, that just makes us relive our trauma and builds anger. That's not a fun place to be. But the song was more than that for me. It was my imagination of how things should have been, and that is what we are going to talk about now. The topic is "Imagine Who You Want to Be."

As a young child, I imagined all the things I wanted from my mom. For me, that meant her staying around instead of dropping me off at the school to be taken care of. It meant her spending time with me, teaching me, and playing with me. Even more critically, it meant she would have stopped my father from hitting me. I loved my father, but he was very physically and verbally abusive. My mom wasn't around to stop him. In the song, I imagine a world where she would be there to protect me.

I realize it sounds strange to choose to believe an imaginary history rather than reality, but the mind of a child often does this. Psychologists refer to this part of abuse as dissociation, when the trauma is so great that the mind protects itself by mentally removing the child from the abusive situation.

Adults may see this as daydreaming or "spacing out," but it is the mind's attempt to protect a developing child from too much mental damage. In my case, I can't remember how the abuse started. I remember how it ended, but I don't remember the middle part. I don't remember the pain, the smell, or the sound. During each episode of abuse, my brain removed those memories. It caused me to wonder if, in those moments, my mind was a blank slate or if it was actually trying to imagine a better world to put myself into.

There were three psychologists who laid the groundwork for European psychology theories. I found Alfred Adler's work the most beneficial because he acknowledged that we have trauma. Yes, bad things have happened to us in the past, but all those things don't decide who we are now. Our present is decided by the decisions we make because of the person we want to be.

In an article by a writer called Mohammed Issa, he talked about how he unintentionally practiced this in his adolescence:

At age eleven, my innocence was shattered due to a coup d'état in Ghana. I had to leave my comfortable, sheltered life, my friends, my school, and my environment. I found myself in a new country, England, with few people like me and few who liked me. I quickly learned that to fit into my new environment meant not to share any dark emotions like fear, shame, grief, or disappointment. I had to show that I was tough, cool, and almost perfect. Simply put, I could not be vulnerable, and I had to close my heart to protect myself. In doing so, I not only closed myself to the dark emotions but also to the lighter ones, and I carried this way of being subconsciously well into my forties.

The facts of my story are true. But I had given it too much significance. At the end, it was just a story that I'd told myself. One that hindered my growth, self-expression, and relationships. True, our past affects our present. True, our past conditioning can influence our behavior today. However, today, I'm suggesting a radical way of thinking. The past itself doesn't matter. Instead, it's the meaning that we attribute to those past events that affects us. Let's look at the traumatic event coldly, empathize with ourselves as to how we were affected in such a way, and then proceed to wipe it out. Let's tell ourselves that the past doesn't matter anymore. Instead, let's focus on what we want and how we will get there.

~~~~~~~~~~~~~~~~

I agree with Adler's teachings as expressed by Mo: "Let's tell ourselves that the past doesn't matter anymore. Instead, let's focus on what we want and how we will get there." Imagine you want to be and find the way to let go of the past to get there.

~~~~~~~~~~~~~~~~

Just as our past affects our present, our past conditioning can influence our behavior today. However, I'm suggesting a radical way of thinking, like Adler and Mo. The past itself doesn't matter. Instead, it's the meaning that we attribute to those past events that affects us.

Look at the traumatic event coldly. Empathize with yourself as to how you were affected, then wipe it out. Let's focus on what we want and how we will get there. Imagine what you want to be and find a way to let go of the past in order to get there. We need to remember that everyone's main goal is simply to be happy.

As a child experiencing trauma, my mind put myself in a place where my world was better—more gentle and kind, more loving. It was thirty years later that my imagination allowed me to write the song, "She," that told that alternate story. I want to stress that my mom and I now have a good relationship. She cannot accept that she allowed bad things to happen to me, but that is her own way of coping. I have decided to feel gratitude for what she did give me, even if some of that is my imagination. Part of that decision was the knowledge that my childhood abuse led to my inability to form close human bonds with others. I needed to leave those feelings behind so I could build lasting connections with my friends and, more importantly, my family, and avoid repeating what happened to me. That perspective drove me to change the way I thought.

There is a powerful movie about the Holocaust called *Life is Beautiful*. It's about a Jewish father who employs his imagination to shield his son from the horrors of the Nazi concentration camp. At the end of the story, it is revealed that the son is the one telling the story, and it shows how grateful he was to his father for shielding and protecting him.

I loved this quote about the movie: "It is about rescuing whatever is good and hopeful from the wreckage of dreams."

My life did not compare to the lives of millions who died in the Holocaust, but I believe that imagination has an amazing ability to change your feelings about a matter. In my case, this meant following the advice of the prior quote to rescue "whatever was good and hopeful from the wreckage of dreams."

My childhood was not good, but as an adult, I could choose to rescue the good and hopeful parts and be grateful rather than resentful. I do this for my quality of life. Feeling resentful is a horribly painful way to live.

I think I understand the reason why I was traumatized by what happened to me—it was because I had no escape. I couldn't do anything to physically get away from the situation that created the trauma. I was only three years old; I was trapped. But like the boy in *Life is Beautiful,* he successfully keeps doing things to get out of every terrible situation by playing a game. It was the hope that he could escape that made the boy believe he would never be caught or trapped.

That hope provided him relief from the trauma, as it did with me, even if it was only imaginary. I imagined who I wanted to be and what life I wanted to live. Children do this naturally, but it can be beaten out of us by the challenges of growing up and just trying to survive.

The world around us likes to kill dreams. Even as adults or young adults, our imagination gives us the ability to intentionally disassociate from nearly anything going on around us, even for just a few seconds, in order to be happy. If you ask every person on earth what they want most, the great majority would simply say, "I want to be happy." Almost every parent would say, "I want my children to be happy."

Reality means that today you may have a lot on your mind, so many things pressing for your attention and limited time, but still, you can imagine a different world.

~~~~~~~~~~~~~~~

Before bringing them into this book, I tried all of the fifteen-second actions I'm suggesting with my family first. There is almost always reluctance and resistance, but we do try them repeatedly. When I came up with this next idea, of doing something silly, we were on the way to Pismo Beach to visit some friends.

We stopped at the Pismo Beach Pier. It was a gorgeous day with sunshine and a soft breeze. There were dozens of surfers in the water, the smell of something cooking on the barbecue, and hundreds of people milling on the pier. In the middle of a bunch of people, we started skipping. Remember doing that as a kid? It took a few seconds for the muscle memory to kick in. We had to decide it was OK for people to laugh and smile at us. Actually, it was better than OK. Part of the goal was to make people smile or laugh, and that is exactly what happened. Not only did a bunch of total strangers smile, but so did all of us. In fact, it worked so well that we did it again a
~~~~~~~~~~~~~~~

few minutes later. I can say with certainty that during those fifteen seconds, I was blissfully, unexplainably happy. I had forgotten every worry or task on my to-do list.

Importantly, the feeling lasted more than fifteen seconds. It lasted all day. Still now, I smile when I talk about it. I would bet that many people who saw us acting silly still remember the crazy family skipping on the Pismo Beach Pier that day.

Once, I was talking with Carlos Santana in the studio when he spontaneously started telling me a story about a man he had seen dancing on the street and how happy it made him feel. That shows you the impact a simple, happy, silly person can make on others.

~~~~~~~~~~~~~~~

I interviewed some people about the thought of acting silly. One person told us they liked making puns, and it made them feel good—even when others didn't laugh. They went on to say that sometimes we take life too seriously. Another person said acting silly feels like freedom and makes them feel like a child again.

Fifteen Seconds to Change Your World

Try to be happy for at least fifteen seconds by doing something silly. Use your imagination to come up with something you can physically do to make you forget your worries. Just be unabashedly joyful. It can be literally anything. If you're in public, you can dance like no one is watching. You can skip. You can wave your arms and hands and give big smiles, and if you're at home, you can do the same thing.
~~~~~~~~~~~~~~~

If you're driving or riding your bike, do some serious in-your-seat dancing. If you're at work, make funny faces at your coworker—just don't get fired!

Whatever you do, be seven years old without a care in the world.

My Fifteen Seconds

For this episode, I went around the house and asked everybody to watch me do a wind dance. If you don't know what that is, it's the dance that the long inflatable tube men do outside the car dealers. They're colorful; they're very tall and long. They look like big, long balloons, and they dance in the wind, so we call it a wind dance.

In general, I'm not a good dancer, but I can proudly say I do a very good wind dance. Not only did I get some good laughs out of my mom and my daughter, but I also successfully invited them to dance with me. In the end, they both agreed that I did the best wind dance.

Citations and references for this chapter are located at the end of the book.

Episodes 5

Letting Go (of Resentment)

One of the first things we learned to say is, "That's unfair." It's a universal feeling that can create resentment if we don't forgive and let things go. It is said that resentment is like drinking a poisoned glass of water and hoping the other person dies.

I was about twenty-three years old and in university when I remember standing outside my boyfriend's window in my hat, boots, and a big coat. It was after class, so it was dark and cold outside. I had walked to his dorm, intending to spend some time with him. I could see from the street that he was likely playing video games, as his window on the sixth floor danced with images reflecting off his monitor. When I called him, he answered and told me he was too busy to spend time with me.

I think that was the day my resentment toward him started growing stronger. Shortly after that, we parted ways. Ten years later, it resulted in some good song material, but those years in between were full of mental stress and pain.

It's remarkable how even small actions in our relationships can have a big impact on our entire lives if we allow them to. And I discovered I had allowed that to happen to me. That relationship that had ended a decade previously was affecting my marriage in the present.

I was thirty-three by the time the realization that I had never really gotten over that relationship hit me. It happened when I saw a picture on social media of him with his wife and new baby. It sent me mentally reeling. It wasn't that I wanted to be in a relationship with him. I was very happy in my own marriage and family. It was the fact that I had never allowed myself to let go of the hurt and pain. The pain from the past was encroaching on my present happiness, even in ways that I never would have guessed.

I wanted to understand my emotions and allow myself to move forward, so I wrote the song "Give Her My Love." The title of the song is a play on words. It's not an attempt to convey my love to another person, like you might say, "Give Susan my love." The song is saying it's OK to give the love I thought belonged to me to the new woman. It's me saying, "I want you to be happy and treat her with the love and tenderness that you didn't give me." Give her my love.

As you listen to the song, you may start to understand where my head and heart were at. This song was a huge step in my healing and helped me to let go of resentment. This song was released in English and Chinese, but I am told my emotions seem more powerful in the Chinese version.

"Give Her My Love"

Before you continue reading, I invite you to experience the song

"Give Her My Love." You can find the song on my YouTube channel (MiistTheSinger) or any streaming platform. I hope you enjoy the song.

To write "Give Her My Love," I had to emotionally go back in time to when I was still with that boyfriend and revisit the memories we had created. I needed to relive that relationship and that part of my life to tell myself it was OK to let go, stop feeling hurt, and be happy. Part of that was going through the mental acknowledgement that he never knew how I felt because I never told him.

In hindsight, I probably never understood why I broke up with him, as the resentment I was harboring inside was just a knot in my stomach and a pain in my heart. The feeling worsened when I was around him, but I didn't know that it was resentment. It was a longing to feel the love and care that I wanted but had never received in the way that I needed.

Again, he didn't know any of this, so the writing of the song was not for him. It was for me—to let him go. Wishing him happy makes me happy, because it releases me from reminiscing on those bad memories and feelings. Through the time I spent with him, I realized he was never the one. He never understood me. He never paid attention to what I needed. He had other priorities.

I'm not saying it was his fault: Sometimes a person is not able to love us the way we need to be loved. As a result, if we don't let go of that relationship or change the dynamic, it is very possible that we would never feel loved in the way we need, simply because that person is not capable of providing it.

There may be several reasons for this, one of them being that I wasn't ready and able to properly receive any kind of love because I didn't love myself. In addition, it seems that he wasn't able to show love to me the way I wanted to feel it. I had to tell myself that was just the reality.

There's no need to hold on to that resentment from not receiving his love. The fact that he didn't love me the way I needed did not mean I wasn't worthy of being loved. It just meant I wasn't going to find it in *that relationship.*

"Give Her My Love" made me realize that what I really wanted was permission from myself to move on and be loved in my current relationship. That was a stunning realization.

Those resulting negative feelings and resentment turned me into a person I didn't like. Just like how drinking that glass of water with poison in it and hoping the other person dies only makes us sick, resentment eventually kills our dreams, compassion, humanity, and self-love.

Once the resentment started, it kept growing, like drinking a little poison every day. Everything he did turned into an internal mental test of his love. To me, the more I felt hurt, the more I wanted not to feel hurt. The more I fought for attention and love, the more resentment I held onto. I would go on to hold that resentment for a decade. Long after he was gone. That is a lot of resentment and hurt.

How did that impact me? In my current relationship, I would find myself reading into situations and assuming my partner or my stepdaughter didn't really love me. In reality, it came from the internal baggage I was still carrying. I'd accepted the self-told message that I was not worthy of love. Even if I was being shown love, I believed it was not real, and it couldn't be trusted.

I didn't like who I was, and if I didn't like who I was, then how could my new family love me? I like the Whitney Houston song, "Greatest Love of All," and it has a lot of truth. I especially like the final stanza: "And if, by chance, that special place that you've been dreaming of leads you to a lonely place, find your strength in love."

She was singing about finding your strength in loving yourself. That's where it starts. You can love yourself by allowing yourself to shed the negative feelings, like the resentment you carry, and the excess baggage that wears your soul down.

~~~~~~~~~~~~~~~~

As I was talking about letting go, what person or issue came to your mind? Was it a close friend, a spouse, or a child? Maybe it was a politician or a boss. Whomever it was, you may not have even thought you were holding resentment towards them until today. Perhaps, though, every time you think of them or see them you feel that ball in the gut of our stomach that says, "I don't really like how that person
~~~~~~~~~~~~~~~~

did ________."

That means you are holding on to resentment. Remember, it is quite likely that the person doesn't even know, and may never know, how you feel. That resentment is only hurting you. Remember the illustration of the poisoned water.

When I wrote "Give Her My Love," it began as pure emotion, without words. When the lyrics were added, it opened my eyes to what I was actually saying. I was telling the guy I had dreamed of marrying and having a family with to give my love to this new woman, a woman I had never met. Even more, it was about my decision to be happy with that. That's obviously a complicated emotion, but I saw it as a necessity because, as a new mom, I understood for the first time what it felt like to love someone unconditionally.

I put myself in his truth. I believed he wanted the same thing for his family and his new baby. When I emotionally let go of him, I didn't want to just let him go and see him repeat the same thing that he did with me. I wanted him to give his partner the love she deserves and give the baby the love she deserves, so they can all be happy. That wish is not only right, but also makes me feel happy to understand I have enough self-love to truly let go of the negative emotions I carried for so long.

I also understood that if I held on to the resentment, I could never truly be happy. Holding onto it made me feel like a victim and like someone did something unjust to me. It felt like he owed me a debt. But he didn't even know it existed, and he would certainly never repay it.

I also know the debt never existed. I had to come to grips with my own illogical thinking to release him and me from the same moment frozen in time. As the famous line in Frozen says, I needed to "let it go." It feels amazing to do that.

Why are we so illogical about resentment? Why can't we see that it hurts us way more than it hurts the other person? I think we hold onto it because we're still hoping to undo whatever wasn't done the way we wished it would have been. We want to believe the failed relationship, the fight, or the hurt was not our fault. If we hold onto that resentment, maybe by some miracle we will be proven right, and the other person will admit they were wrong. But if they don't even know about it, what's the likelihood of that happening?

Even if the other person is so callous and unloving that they intentionally hurt us, why do we want to poison ourselves by holding on to resentment? Is our holding on to all the poison hurting the other person at all?

If they're that mean and selfish, they are not thinking of us, so the resentment still only hurts us in those sad situations. Appreciating and loving ourselves and cultivating other healthy relationships might be the only solution. If you're in that horrible situation, find someone to give you a hug or give yourself a big hug and say, "It's OK to let it go. I choose not to drink this poison. I'm going to put that glass down and move forward the best I can."

How do we mentally overcome that when we know a great injustice has been done to us? In my case, it was when it became clear that my resentment was eroding my present happiness and, in essence, stealing from my future happiness. The righteous indignation I felt, whether right or wrong, wasn't worth that price. It was more valuable to me to have the happiness.

I'm not saying that it is OK for a mean, unloving person to make us feel unloved. It's not OK. However, I am saying: Let's not allow that person to impact our happiness for the rest of our lives. It is the understanding that we have value, and we deserve to be happy and feel loved. So it's OK to seek happiness again. Do not allow what someone did to you to define your happiness or your ability to feel love. It's important. Whatever it takes, we need to let it go. It's for our own benefit. It's not for the other person.

During my interviews on resentment, I asked one group what forgiveness meant to them. They answered that relationships aren't made by avoiding conflict, but by working through that conflict with someone. Although you don't owe anyone forgiveness, it shows the depth of your care for them. They also said that many people feel that forgiveness is weakness, but they felt that it was the opposite— strength. In their words, it "means you're a part of something that's worth continuing..." and although it's hard, it's a way to get closure for yourself.

We later interviewed the same group about gratefulness, which you can listen to here. Link the interviews.

Fifteen Seconds to Change Your World

Start by saying it out loud: "I feel resentment toward ______ because they ________." Whatever it is, verbalize it.

You may find that saying it out loud causes you to realize you really don't want that baggage anymore. You may start shedding it right there, or it may give you enough strength to talk to the other person about why you feel the way you do.

In any case, the beginning of solving a problem is acknowledging that it exists.

My Fifteen Seconds

I realized that I still need to work on the relationship with my dad. So, for this fifteen-second action, I said to myself, "I feel resentment toward my dad because he left me and my mom over thirty years ago." It was tough to hear my own voice say those words, but it felt really good.

Citations and references for this chapter are located at the end of the book.

Episode 6

Change Your World in 15 Seconds

I listened to a podcast recently about the dangers of social media and how unhealthy it is for us. After one hour of listening, the host suggested we remove our social media apps and disconnect. Go cold turkey. I thought to myself, "Yes, that is what we all should do, but very few—including me—are likely to do it." It felt like too big an ask.

I feel the same way when I hear about so many of the huge issues we face as a human family. My heart and mind want to do something to help, but it's always overwhelming to try to figure out where to begin. When that happens, I shut down or ignore it because I don't want to feel powerless, but I also know doing nothing doesn't really help anyone.

So, I started thinking and talking to my family and friends about how to not be overwhelmed. Like you, I want to do positive actions, something to help, but they need to be achievable, simple, and powerful.

That is how the theme of *Make Me Smile* came about, to "Change Your World in Fifteen Seconds." The ultimate goal is to change the

way we look at each other, including ourselves, in a very literal sense—
to be more connected, kinder, to show that we care about each other,
and to show that we care about ourselves.

We as a human family have forgotten many of these actions that
take very little effort, but are very powerful, actions like smiling, being
grateful, or reminding someone you love them. It takes surprisingly
little time to do some pretty amazing stuff, even to call someone and
say, "I just wanted to tell you, I love you. Have a good day." It takes
very little time, but imagine how it would make that person feel.

That twelve-second phone call might keep that person going for a
day, a week, or a month, and it costs us nothing. It affects us, as well.
We feel good, making someone else happy and knowing that we made
a connection that day. There are dozens of fifteen-second actions we
can do. That is what we're trying to achieve together.

As part of this idea, we're providing a Kindness Kube® on my
website, on a donation basis, that has five of these actions on it. The
cube is designed to be placed on your desk, vanity, or nightstand.
Each morning when you wake up, you pick a side of the cube and
do that action. Each action takes only fifteen seconds, doesn't cost
anything, and is powerful. At the end of the day, the Kindness Kube™
is there to ask you how you did each day.

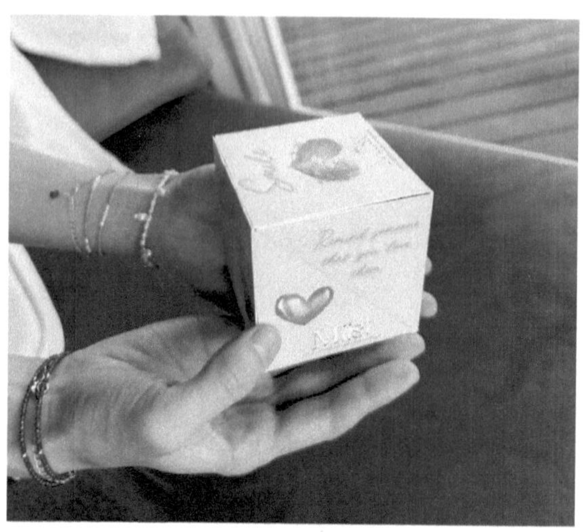

The Kindness Kube™ by Miist. Available on a donation basis at www.miistthesinger.com/podcast

The goal is to just do one thing, but as we get into the practice of it, we may choose to do more, and that's even better. However, do not make it overwhelming. The idea is to make it simple and achievable.

You may be wondering at this point what this has to do with a song. A little while ago, Narada Michael Walden was mentoring me. If you don't know who Narada is, you definitely know the artists he produced: Whitney Houston, Mariah Carey, Aretha Franklin, Wham!, Carlos Santana, and dozens more. He is one of the greatest producers in the world. I'm very grateful that he discovered me in late 2023 and produced my debut album, The Songs from the Living Room, in 2024.

He would often send me home to write new songs. He would pick a genre or tell me what kind of music he wanted me to create. On this particular day, he had played me a disco dance beat, and he told me to write something on it. I imagined a song that Dua Lipa would perform and began writing.

The song I wrote ended up being called "Move Your Body Slowly." It was very upbeat and fun, but without a lot of message to it. He then surprised me and insisted I sing it. If I were going to do that, I needed to revise the song to fit my values of having a meaningful message. So while it is still a fun song, and one of my biggest commercial hits, it also has a special message. The beginning of the music video starts with the words: "Sometimes, no matter how crazy the world is around you, all you want to do is slow dance with the one you love." As you listen to the song, listen to the story it's telling.

<u>"Move Your Body Slowly"</u>

Before you continue reading, I invite you to experience the song "Move Your Body Slowly." You can find the song on my YouTube channel (MiistTheSinger) or any streaming platform.

When I was writing my version of the song, I pictured myself walking into a party where everyone, including me, was dancing and having a good time. I was in the middle of the dance floor when my husband walked into the room and I locked eyes with him. I found myself wanting nothing more than to slow dance with him. So, the way I imagined it, while everyone else was jumping and dancing to a crazy beat, my husband and I were in the middle, slow dancing.

The message of the song is to have fun and be present in the moment. The world is crazy. Our lives are crazy. It seems our minds are always engaged, but when we feel that need for a real connection, we need to slow down and be present in the moment. That is what the fifteen-second messages are all about. Each fifteen-second action forces our mind to be present in a world full of distractions. It is very important for us to find a few moments each day to be present because that is what makes life truly enjoyable. That is what makes it precious and incredibly beautiful. Otherwise, we might as well be robots.

Our cultures and commercial systems push us to achieve higher education, make money, and be famous or powerful. But when we are at the end of our lives, does any of that matter? What memories do we dwell on after all is said and done? It rarely has to do with things or achievements. What *really* counts for most of us is living a meaningful and fulfilling life.

There have been several studies about people who have had near-death experiences. It is speculated that in the very last seconds of life, the mind often does what is called a life review. Dr. Ajmal Zemmar, a neurosurgeon from the University of Louisville, talked about this when he theorized that when a person is dying, "Their brains may be replaying some of the nicest moments they experienced in their lives."

Consider what your life review would be made up of? Would it be the degree you earned, the new car, the video game, the diamond jewelry, or your hundred million social media followers? Or would it be the love you felt, the smiles you shared, the laughter, the friends, the beauty of a special moment, and the times you felt safe, at peace, and loved?

~~~~~~~~~~~~~~~

To discover each of the fifteen-second call-to-actions, I found the question to be, "What should be the most important things in our lives, and how can we make more of those moments?" When we find what those truly meaningful moments are, we need to prioritize *doing* them. We need to be present, especially for those whom you love and who love you, including yourself. I want to do the really important things on a daily basis. The ones I will remember when I'm older, as I'm reflecting on my life. How about you?

~~~~~~~~~~~~~~~

At the beginning of this episode, I talked about the podcaster who told us to delete all the social media apps. I admit when I heard her, I mentally put off that suggestion. That's not unusual. When we perceive something to be too difficult to do, we rarely follow through on it. So, I got to thinking about what would be a reasonable thing to ask, something that I would do right away, and that others would be willing to do. It would need to be something simple, powerful, and fulfilling, but also achievable for a commitment-phobic world.

That was the decision process for "fifteen seconds." A ridiculously small amount of time, which I felt every single person on earth could afford. If we actually did it, you and I together, it would change our world.

That was a high bar to set for actions that would take such small amounts of time; however, after writing down dozens of ideas for the *Make Me Smile* podcast, I became even more certain that fifteen seconds was enough time to achieve those goals. It was short enough so that no one could say, "I don't have the time," and long enough to enact life-changing actions like smiling, showing gratitude, being thankful, acting silly, and reminding someone you love them.

In fact, I found it remarkable that the most powerful actions were often those that took less than fifteen seconds of time. Of course, not all of them, but remarkably, we can do an *awful* lot to change our world in fifteen seconds.

That podcast I listened to about social media had a really big ask. I'm also going to ask you to do something about social media, but it will be a very small ask. I'm not going to ask you to delete anything or to stop doing anything, but I'd like you to really try this next time before you click on that social media app or go to that website. Pause for fifteen seconds and think about something else. For those fifteen seconds, think about what you are grateful for. It could be a person, an animal, your mind or body, a flower, or a sunset. Anything that you feel grateful for today. That's it. Then, if you feel the need to open that app, go ahead.

~~~~~~~~~~~~~~~

At its most basic, gratefulness is known to release dopamine, which
~~~~~~~~~~~~~~~

makes you feel happier, reduces anxiety and depression, and gives us hope. Social media also produces dopamine, but in an unhealthy way. When you go on social media, your dopamine spikes. It spikes because your brain is anticipating that you are going to have fun.

The longer you are on social media—the more swipes, the more clicks, the more dopamine—it loses its effect. You feel driven to swipe and click more and more, yet you get less and less of an effect. So, you sit there for hours, doing something that in the end fails to deliver on its promise to make you happy.

Dr. Anna Lemke, expert on addiction and author of *Dopamine Nation*, calls the smartphone the modern-day hypodermic needle. We turn to it for quick hits, seeking attention, validation, and distraction with each swipe, like, and tweet. But it is important to understand what we're actually looking for to understand the problem and the solution. The phone and the social media apps have an implicit promise: "Open me, and you will have fun." The problem is, how many times do we find ourselves really happy after surfing for thirty minutes, forty-five minutes, or longer? The promise goes mostly unfulfilled, but that tantalizing promise is still there the next time with the same result, and we keep coming back.

We know that phones and social media can cause us to become withdrawn and disconnected from each other. So then why do we keep going back to them? What are we really looking for subconsciously? What are we really after? It must be something like hunger, thirst, the desire for love, hardwired human desires that, if unfulfilled, make us unhappy. The promise that social media makes must appeal to the most basic human need. Otherwise, we wouldn't keep trying to get something from it that we never actually get. It took me quite a while to find the answer. I had multiple conversations with my friends, trying to understand what the real promise of social media is, and when it finally occurred to me, I was shocked that I didn't know it.

Many of us carry anxiety, fear, and pain. This might come from our past, our present, or even because of the world's current state. Society at large encourages isolation, and all those feelings make us want to withdraw, which is the opposite of what we need. The human condition requires connection, and we cannot feel happy without that connection.

As communities grow wealthier, they move from community buildings to houses, then to houses with gates. From there, we arrive at lockout communities, then mansions with servants. Eventually, we find ourselves all alone with our wealth and our unhappiness.

We have trained ourselves to fight the beautiful inclination to share, to connect, and to touch another human. Our children are not immune to that either. Instead of playing outside with each other, our children play video games at home, and while they may do that with others, contact via electronics is not necessarily a connection. It often fosters the opposite—isolation.

Loneliness feels like no one loves us enough to reach out. It feels like we are not worth loving. We may even try to tell ourselves that's not true, but loneliness makes it feel true.

We talked to people walking the streets, starting the conversation by reminding them that 50 percent of adults in the U.S. admit they are lonely. Some were well aware of this, while others were shocked to hear the statistic. One person we interviewed suggested reaching out to loved ones when you notice they seem lonely, to check on how they're doing. The general consensus was that interactions with the surrounding community are important to combat loneliness, even with people you see during your routine errands.

Another person we talked to brought up the effect texting has and explained how they had taken back control of that by turning off their notifications. Texting is not a social interaction, but it's disguised as one, causing a lot of misunderstandings.

Think about this for a moment with me: Humans are made to be connected. It is a basic need, just like eating, drinking, sleeping, and love. By definition, social media is supposed to be "social," but that's a loose definition of what it is. It's supposed to connect us, but does it really?

In the next chapter, I'll talk more about this theme and finish telling you about my surprising discovery.

Fifteen Seconds to Change Your World

So here is our fifteen-second call to action for this episode. For fifteen seconds, right now, we are going to think about what we are grateful for. There are some guidelines here. Please don't include man-made things or ideas. In other words, don't be grateful for having a ton of social media followers, a PhD, or a large bank account. Think about things in nature, human relationships that you have, things you like about yourself, or something you really enjoy, like food, exercise, music, or touch. Things that would appear in your Life Review.

My Fifteen Seconds

For my fifteen seconds, I thought of my daughter. She has brought a lot of laughter into my life, and I've learned a lot from her, including how to love. I'm thankful for her being so patient with me.

Citations and references for this chapter are located at the end of the book.

Episode 7

The (Failed) Promise of Social Media

In this chapter, I'll be finishing up my thoughts from the previous one about the promise of social media and how it influences human connection in the world today.

Humans need to be connected. Whether we realize it or not, our minds and bodies crave being part of the world around us. Both consciously and subconsciously, we look for ways to make those connections.

Much like the way we become hungry or thirsty, our bodies start subtly telling us something is a little bit wrong when we are not connected. When we're hungry, at the beginning, it isn't a loud voice yelling at us. It's a subtle hint that we don't feel quite right and that we might want to get a bite to eat.

Our need for connection works the same way that hunger does. When we don't satisfy our hunger, the voice gets louder and more insistent, up to a point where it's at its worst. In our house, we call that being "hangry." When our bodies signal that we need something, we pursue that need either subconsciously or consciously. Neglecting to fulfill this need properly has consequences.

You have choices as to how you feed that need. For instance, when you're hungry, you can eat junk food and feel full. But what would happen if you ate nothing but junk food? Lacking nutrition, your body would start to break down. It would affect your sleep, relationships, ability to work, and your happiness. Finally, that type of "food" makes your body susceptible to sickness and shortens your life. Even though we may know this, our minds can trick us. We start craving junk food and the quick high it gives us. A large amount of sugar, glucose, and bad cholesterol tastes great and releases dopamine, simultaneously killing us slowly.

Of course, most of us eat a bit of junk food, and our bodies are OK. It is not so much that a little junk food will hurt us, but the lack of nutritious food will. This is the same as feeding our minds on too much social media. Social media promises a quick and easy way to connect. I mean, it's in the very name. What could go wrong?

Social media triggers and spikes dopamine. Small doses and limited interaction with it have limited negative effects. That being said, too much of it and going too long without finding a real connection will eventually make us lose our happiness, compassion, and humanity. It is insidious, like junk food, though our brains want it. We don't even realize what it's doing until we have diabetes or heart disease and are left wondering what happened. Just like junk food initially tastes good, social media initially tastes good to our emotions.

Did you know that people suffering from starvation go through phases where the hunger pains get louder and louder until they don't feel them any longer?

It made me wonder what a world would look like if we reached the point where, as a human society, we were so starved for real connection that we no longer felt the need for it. We could become a world detached from humanity, with people unable to communicate productively, divided into antisocial units of society.

In my song, "Could You Lend Me a Smile," the twenty-year-old man died alone. That experience has become so common that they have a term for it: lonely death. Could it have been prevented? Could it *be* prevented in the future?

I say that it not only *could* be, but it *must* be. However, it takes you and me to put in a little effort.

Toward the end of "Could You Lend Me a Smile," the voices of hope, the cello and violin, start moving toward him, symbolizing other humans who hear his pleas for help. You can feel the hope in the swelling of those voices at the end of the song. However, the voices fade away, and only he remains standing there because he starts to doubt whether what he felt was real or imagined.

<u>"Could You Lend Me a Smile (Spoken Word)"</u>

Previously, I shared the English version of this song, but I'd like to share a special version featuring Michael Ursu. This version is spoken word and tells the full story of the Japanese salaryman who died alone.

Hope is powerful, but even more so when there is a reason to hope. My dream was that the man found a reason to hope because you and I started smiling at him again—but that depends on us reaching out to him with our smiles and kindness.

The most precious life experiences are created through connection, whether that is with loved ones, animals, the earth, or even ourselves. Connection helps us feel loved, like we are a part of something bigger, and to feel understood and supported. The only way to get these basic human needs is to form bonds. The bonds start with simple actions like smiling and feeling gratitude.

As humans, we always like shortcuts, so when we hear the promise of being able to instantly make easy connections, we dive in. The promise of community and bonding is why we get on social media to laugh together, cry together, and share our thoughts and feelings. It is called "social" media, and we are social creatures.

We're sold the lie that we will become a community, one that values each other's thoughts, and that it will give us a voice with like-minded individuals. In reality, social media is all one-way "connections." We can't form a truly lasting bond with a picture, even if that picture is of a person telling us what we want to hear. There is no one making eye contact, no one smiling at us, and giving tactile feedback. There is no two-way bond forming.

The only way we truly connect is through human interactions like smiling, talking, sharing, and loving. That is what truly satisfies our need for connection, and that is what the "Fifteen Seconds to Change Your World" tips are all about. It is a place to start, and a chance to rebuild what we have lost—a chance to change our world by becoming a community.

It's disturbing that people don't recognize the lack of real community in the world today. I spoke previously about being in Monterey, trying to get people to talk about smiling at one another. It was incredibly difficult and almost discouraging. Most people wouldn't even acknowledge us. Our daughter, standing about fifty feet away, said people were making fun of us for trying to engage people in smiling. That convinces me even more that we must change the way we look at each other. Some of us are so far removed from healthy and normal human connections that we make fun of those who ask for it, yet *every single human* requires connection to feel fulfilled.

Not everything that happened during that visit was negative. We did meet a few happy, smiling people who were engaging and kind. The majority of the people there were on vacation, experiencing one of the most beautiful places on Earth, yet they looked mad at the world. In comparison, the number of obviously happy people was noticeably small.

Speaking of beautiful places on Earth, while we were in Monterey, we visited the Monterey Bay Aquarium. It's an amazing place, one that my family and I love to visit. While I was there, I noticed something unusual.

I heard all of the usual "ooh," "aah," and children excitedly saying, "Mom, Dad! Look at this!" I saw enormous smiles and the buzz of excitement.

Something else was noticeably *missing*. There was nearly no one on their phones. Everyone had their heads up, looking around at each other and the amazing animals. Not even the teenagers had their phones out. It was like we were all a part of a sacred adventure, now free from the outside world. All of this was a bit ironic—I had to type out these thoughts on my phone, which means I was the only person there using a phone. It brought me hope.

When we feel connected to animals and to life itself in all their crazy, awe-inspiring forms, we don't feel the need to seek connection through social media or video games. The implicit promise of fun and connection that those apps and games promise couldn't compete with what was in front of our eyes: nature, in all its glory. We felt connected. Even in the cafeteria, when everyone was taking a break, there were very few phones out. However, once you went back out to the street, there were phones in hand everywhere.

The lesson here is remarkable: The stronger our connection with nature, animals, humans, and ourselves, the less we feel the need to be on social media. We turn to social media for the false, implicit promise of connection and happiness, but science shows that being outdoors and appreciating nature increases happiness and connection and decreases screen time.

The most amazing documentary, called *My Octopus Teacher*, tells the story of a man who discovers a wild octopus during his daily ocean explorations. Over a period of months, they form an incredible bond. It was stunning and touching. Watching that made me feel like we were meant to be stewards of this incredible planet, and it emphasized the bond we have with nature. When we're connected to nature, we become less and less drawn to artificial means of connection.

Can you imagine that man deciding to take a day off so that he could surf the internet for a day instead of seeing his octopus friend? It is a ludicrous choice, right? Yet, many of us make the same wrong choice every day.

Our basic human need to feel connected is no different than hunger, thirst, or the need for love. We need connection to each other, the very ground we stand on, the incredible animals surrounding us, and the amazing architecture of this planet.

We stand in awe at high mountains, serene lakes, or ocean waves pounding against the shore. It is widely known that putting your hands in the earth and working with it, or going for a walk by the ocean, produces oxytocin. That's the love hormone. We're designed to be connected to the Earth, and we're designed to be connected to each other and the animals. That's why we get such positive feelings when we spend time in nature, playing with animals, or being in awe of the Earth.

When was the last time you spent an hour in nature, with your dog, or with your loved ones, and afterward felt it was wasted time?

When was the last time you spent an hour surfing on your phone and later felt you just lost an hour of your life to a screen?

Perhaps surprisingly, there are many animals that need connection. Even animals that you wouldn't think of needing a connection. One article tells the story of a sunfish in a Japanese aquarium, which had shut down to undergo renovations. The sunfish became withdrawn and stopped eating. Someone wondered if the sunfish felt lonely, so they put photos of human faces on the glass. They even hung uniforms on racks in clear view of the sunfish. The sunfish became more lively and even started eating again. Evidently, the sunfish was lonely.

Zoo animals that live in so-called natural habitats are noticeably more active and more responsive than those in concrete jungles. My dog will run across a hundred yards of concrete to the smallest patch of dirt to do her business on earth. She loves grass and the forest. She hates cities and sidewalks. Why do all these creatures need a connection with our earth and each other? Can we learn something from that about our needs and how best to satisfy them?

In our last chapter, I challenged you to spend fifteen seconds thinking about things you have reason to be grateful for. We're going to do the same thing in this chapter. I mentioned that for those fifteen seconds of gratitude, we must think about things in the natural world, not things that are manmade or created, like having a ton of social media followers, a PhD, a large bank account, or fame. Why?

Being grateful for those manmade ideals doesn't work. Those ideals don't connect us with our world, nor with each other. They may have a use and practical value. They may make us feel more important. As far as feeling connected, they're neutral at best, but often negative. We feel connected, satisfied, and emotionally full when we are connected to other humans, ourselves, or nature. Everything else may be temporarily fun or pleasurable, but the happiness they give does not last.

I want to bring back to your mind the life review theory. What moments of happiness would we reflect on during our last breaths? The number of social media followers we have, the advanced degrees, the billions in our bank account, and the fame we gained? Or would it be the love we felt, the friendships we built, and the hugs or smiles we received? The latter is what makes us feel purpose and true happiness, and that is what we try to achieve with the fifteen seconds of gratitude.

We need time daily to recharge, letting go of accumulated troubles, stress, pressure, and the crazy lives we lead. Many times, we go to our social media apps to achieve that, but does it really recharge us? Have you ever plugged in your device and discovered after a few hours that it wasn't actually charging? So you start messing with the cable, and it does that little *ding ding!* You see that lightning bolt symbol come on and off, on and off as you mess with it. It's frustrating when your phone comes away *not* recharged, isn't it? It's the same way with us. When we attempt to recharge by plugging into ideals created by men, like social media, video games, or fame and power, we expect to feel recharged. We hope to feel fulfilled. Yet we most often come away empty, low on energy, or drained—not fulfilled or happy, and certainly not feeling like we have found purpose in life. Those artificial promises of fulfillment and contentment do not give us what we hope for.

There's a saying in English: "My eyes are satisfied." Google said that phrase means that someone has seen something so visually pleasing or beautiful that they feel completely content and have no desire to see anything else.

Have you ever felt that way about social media? We feel connected when there is a two-way connection. You and I need to get back to basic human needs. We need to connect with ourselves, the people around us, and our natural world. Let's start with that—you and me. We can change the way we look at each other.

~~~~~~~~~~~~~~~

In my interview for this chapter, I spoke to Katleen, a French-American singer-songwriter. At the time, she was competing on *The Voice* in France and estimated she'd been working full-time in music for about eight years. Even before I prompted her, she started naming things she was grateful for: her friends, family, and the rest of her support system. Some of these people had even flown out to support her in France. Realizing how much love they had for her made her feel emotional, especially in a career that, in her words, is "filled with a lot of highs and a lot of lows." I noted that she was grateful for the connection she had with the people in her life, not the fame she was receiving.

Fifteen Seconds to Change Your World

So, for the next fifteen seconds, think about what you are grateful for today or this week. It can be a flower you saw, a friend, or your favorite meal. Perhaps you enjoy a beautiful sunrise—or maybe you're more like me and love the sunset. Whatever it is, pause for fifteen seconds and ponder what you feel grateful for.
~~~~~~~~~~~~~~~

My Fifteen Seconds

I'm grateful for all the flowers that are out this season. There are a lot of them I can't name off the top of my head, but as I write this, it's early spring. A lot of flowers are just coming out. Some I know that are in my yard are on the lemon tree, and some are on the plum tree. When I go on walks, I like to gently touch them, too. I know not all connections need to be physical, but touching the flowers makes me feel connected to them in a special way. It allows me to know another aspect of them.

It seems that we inherently know what we should be grateful for. So next time you reach out to that app, please pause for fifteen seconds to think about what you are grateful for. You might just feel like putting down your phone.

Citations and references for this chapter are located at the end of the book.

Episode 8

Remember Me Again

About fifteen years ago, I found myself in love with a young man who attended my university. I use "in love" loosely, from the perspective of a twenty-two-year-old who didn't know herself yet. Like so many young loves, that relationship had its challenges, but even to this day, I know that relationship was transformative. Perhaps it is the rose-colored glasses of hindsight, but I believe it was more than just a crush.

A decade later, I found myself in a different life, in a different country, and on another continent. And then I saw an announcement that he was getting married. Talk about mixed emotions! Immediately, I was taken back to our relationship, with all of its good times— laughter, companionship, having a shoulder to lean on—and the bad times, like the breakup and broken heart. While recovering from that, I had a lot of doubts about the good memories I had. But the thought I kept returning to was whether he remembered me. I mean, I know he remembered who I was, but did he remember me? Did he think of me? Did he wonder where I was and what I was doing? If I were happy or sad?

I felt weird wondering these things, since it shouldn't matter—but it did matter. I didn't want to be forgotten. I wanted to be special and to know that I made an impression he would carry the rest of his life. I didn't want him to be sad about me, but when he drank the same kind of drink that I had once brought him, or when he ate our favorite meal, I wanted him to have the whisper of me in his mind. I wanted my memory to be like a fragrance passing in the breeze, triggering a childhood memory.

I would never admit that to him, and I hope neither he nor his wife listened when I spoke about this on my podcast. But I don't think my feelings are that unusual. After all, men and women have been trying to be remembered throughout history. It is why we name stadiums, libraries, streets, and landmarks after people. Even mountains and scientific discoveries are named after people who are long gone. We want to be remembered.

So, I did the only thing I know that helps me process emotions. I wrote a song. It's called "Remember Me Again," and it was on my 2024 album, *The Songs from the Living Room*. The song includes these lyrics:

Remember me again when your lips kiss your lover
Remember me again when the sunset drips like silver
Remember me again when the night turns into whispers
Remember me again when your dreams melt into dawn

We filmed the music video for "Remember Me Again" in a studio that looked like an old house from the 1940s. The actors played my old boyfriend and his wife, doing various things around the house that matched the lyrics and just living life.

Each scene includes a déjà vu moment in which the actor playing my old boyfriend catches a glimpse of me, or a reflection triggered by a sound or moment. I appear, then quickly disappear. At one point, the videographer asked me to laugh like I was haunting him with my memories, but that wasn't correct. I didn't want to haunt him. I didn't want him to be miserable and unable to live a happy life. I don't want him to love me more than he loves his wife.

I just don't want to be forgotten. I want to be special enough that I'm worth remembering. I don't want to be just another face in an ocean of faces. None of us does. It never feels good when you run into someone who made an impression on you, and they obviously don't remember you, right?

The music video's story is hard to explain without you seeing it, but you can see it on YouTube or my website. I loved filming that music video, and I hope you enjoy it, too. It was produced by one of the greatest record producers of all time, Narada Michael Walden, who has multiple GRAMMY®s, EMMY®s, and fifty-seven number one hits.

<u>"Remember Me Again"</u>

Use the code below to watch this music video and listen to this song, full of my feelings about wanting to be remembered. If you prefer to search for it yourself, it's available on my YouTube channel (MiistTheSinger) or any streaming platform.

Even now, when I listen to that song, I think about that old relationship, but today I find myself wondering... after you listened to the song, who did you think of?

~~~~~~~~~~~~~~~~

The desire to be remembered is a universal human emotion going back thousands of years. In the ancient Hebrew language, there is a word, *"zakar."* It is often translated "to remember" in English, but it means more than that. It means remembering with the intent to do something about it. It was used when servants of God asked to be remembered for being faithful. It wasn't just a request to be thought of kindly in hindsight; rather, it conveyed the idea that God would remember them and act on that memory by bringing them back to life. This concept exists in the Bible and other religious books. The idea is that people would live their lives in such a way to be worthy of being remembered, so much so that they would be brought back to life.

In essence, that is what naming a mountain or river after a human does, at least superficially. It gives a kind of immortality to that person, or at least a semblance of it. Bridges, mountains, and libraries named after people have the same intent to carry on one's name. It keeps them alive in people's memories, so that in some small way, they remain alive even after they are long gone.
~~~~~~~~~~~~~~~~

There are people throughout history who are remembered for spectacular achievements. Albert Einstein, Gandhi, Cleopatra, Jesus—you recognize these names. Other people become immortalized by doing awful things. When you hear names such as Charles Manson, Adolf Hitler, or Jack the Ripper, those people's names are remembered for very different reasons.

There is a difference between remembering a name in history and remembering someone who meant something personally to you. Can you think of someone you loved dearly that you have lost? That remembering, the longing and desire to be with them again, is very different than remembering a historical figure.

It got me thinking. Who do we really want to be remembered by? What do we want to be remembered *for*, and how can this idea of wanting to be remembered help us to live a better, more fulfilling life now? By fulfilling, I mean filling that hole we all feel inside—the desire to be wanted, loved, and needed. The desire to have a purpose and a true reason for being alive.

In past *Make Me Smile* chapters, I talked about the idea of a life review. It's the theory that, in the last moments of life, our minds recall our life's highlights so that we can feel a sense of peace before we pass. In those last moments of life, what do you think you would like to remember? What would help you feel calm and peaceful? Would it be that TikTok dance that went viral in 2020—or was that 2021... or 2022? Would it be winning the lottery, carrying the world's best something trophy in 1999 (or was that 2001)? Can you even remember who won that trophy last year or who won the most gold medals at the 2020 Olympics?

Perhaps for some, that is what they would choose to remember. For me, I think in those final moments, I want to remember holding the people I love. I want to remember being held, hearing the laughter of my family and friends, and loving with all my heart. I don't need a stadium named after me or a hundred number one hits. Rather, as a famous song indicated, the greatest thing in life is to feel and give love.

That song "Nature Boy" was sung by Nat King Cole, but I didn't remember that; I just remembered the lyrics that resonated with my heart.

I wonder how many of us have truly learned that. Or are we still thinking that the greatest thing is our fame, wealth, power, or intelligence and station in life?

When it all comes down to those final moments, what really is the greatest thing? As corny as it sounds, what is the point of anything? If we do not feel loved and have no one to love, we can sit in our mansions, drive our fancy cars, and party all night long, every night, trying to convince ourselves that those things make us happy. But that is just not the way we're made.

I'm not saying there is no satisfaction in a job well done. Whether we are teachers or are building a company, those life choices are who we are, and they give color to our lives. However, they're not the purpose of our life. It's kind of like a hamburger. To make a great hamburger, you need a bun, maybe some lettuce, tomato, pickles, and perhaps ketchup or special sauce. Those are all complementary to the meal, but without the patty, there is no hamburger.

There are many options to enhance our lives. Our work, the example we set, the children we raise, and the contribution to our communities are all complementary to our lives, but love is the "patty."

It reminds me of the old hamburger commercial, "Where's the beef?" In the hamburger of life, we need to know "where's the beef?" (I apologize to the vegetarians out there.) Love is the beef; our need to be loved and to love someone else is our most basic and powerful need. Without it, we will turn the world upside down to find it. The lack of love can literally break our hearts, and the power of love has proven stronger than even the power of life. In our day-to-day lives, showing love and being remembered matter. Smiling, kindness, and gratitude matter.

~~~~~~~~~~~~~~~~

For this chapter's interviews, I spoke again to Katleen. She told me she'd been working on some cool new projects, including both French and English songs. She'd also been exploring genres, textures, and styles within her music. She spoke about how her style has evolved over time and how being a musician gave her the freedom to try whatever her heart called her to.

I asked her what she wanted to be remembered for. She said, "This is why I do music. It's to touch people's souls and impact them in a positive way, and maybe that's making them feel not alone... whatever was bothering them that day, it's made it better."

~~~~~~~~~~~~~~~~

I know this chapter was a bit heavy, but I hope it gave you something to think about. It certainly made me think about living in such a way that the people I come into contact with will remember me because I remembered them. I noticed them. They were not just faces passing by; they were people with lives, concerns, burdens, and joys. I want to become a person who touches their lives, even if only for a second.

Touching other people's lives and feeling connected is what makes us feel better. It helps you and me today and helps us change our world in the long term. This is not some fictional fantasy world. This is basic human psychology. It is not a new revelation. It is a reminder for all of us that we need to find a new way to look at each other.

If you catch yourself thinking one person can't make a difference, think about this: If I smile at you today, and we each smile at a person tomorrow, and the four of us smile at a person on the third day, and so on... by day thirty-three, we will have collectively smiled at everyone on Earth. The entire world. All it takes is one person to join each person every day. Do you think the world would be a better place in thirty-three days if everyone on Earth started to smile at each other?

~~~~~~~~~~~~~~~~

In my yard, there is a lemon tree. It grows the most unusual lemons, and I'll be talking about that in the next chapter.

Speaking of the lemon tree reminded me of one of our family's favorite books. It's called *A Coconut Named Bob*. I would like to read a few pages:
~~~~~~~~~~~~~~~~

On a sun-drenched island lived a lonely little boy. He had a few friends besides his dad and the fishermen on the wharf. Most of the time, he worked for the fishermen, selling their catch in the market. When there were no fish to sell, he gathered coconuts the way his father had taught him.

He walked along the beach until he found the right tree, then he climbed its rough trunk. Sitting among the branches, he picked coconuts one by one and threw them down to the sand below. One day, as the boy was working in a tree, a certain coconut caught his eye. He twisted it loose, turned it around and around, looking closely at it. Somehow, he knew there was something special about this coconut. He put it aside and continued his work. When the boy was finished, he slid down the tree and loaded all the coconuts into a burlap bag. He headed to the market and sold every coconut—but one.

He ran home tired but eager. Under the setting sun, he took the coconut behind his house and set it on a log. He disappeared into a weathered old shed and came out holding two cans of paint. The boy pried the lid off a can of red paint, dipped his brush into it, and gave the coconut a mouth. Next, he grabbed a can of green paint and painted two round eyes.

He looked closely at the coconut's new face and, smiling, he whispered, "Your name is Bob."

Fifteen Seconds to Change Your World

Take fifteen seconds to define who you are. Doing that will help you see if the current you is who you really want to be. If not, you may need to adjust your course to be the person you were meant to be—a person who is memorable and worthy of being remembered while you are alive, not just after your death. Describe who you are. Start with "I am" and finish the sentence.

I'm going to give you a hint before we do this. There is a game my husband plays at dinner parties. He calls it "describe who you are in six words." It can be any six words, whatever has meaning to you. There are no rules here. Just describe who you are.

You might be feeling like you need more than fifteen seconds. The idea of the fifteen seconds here is to say what comes to your mind first, as this is generally how we truly think of ourselves. But, by all means, think about this throughout the day.

Most people will end the phrase "I am" with a title—mother, driver, CEO, musician—because we are taught to think of ourselves that way. Might it be better to describe ourselves with more descriptive words about who we are as a person? Things like "I am a good friend" or "I am a good person." Maybe, "I love deeply." What do you think?

Whatever your answer was, ask yourself if that answer is what you want it to be. If not, now might be the time to start making small changes. The world tries to convince us that the most important things in life are money, fame, education, and power. In reality, the most important and valuable things are those that make us feel connected to each other.

Being someone who lights up the world around us simply because we care enough to try—*that* would be a wonderful legacy to have. I want to be a person like that, one who is worthy of being remembered, not just after I pass, but every day for the rest of my life. I hope you join me in that quest.

My Fifteen Seconds

I am music. I am surrounded by love. I am having a lot of fun.

Citations and references for this chapter are located at the end of the book.

Episode 9

The Lemon Tree: Personification and the Need for Connection

At the front of our house, between the garage and the front door, we have a lemon tree. It's about ten feet tall and has branches that extend about four feet from its trunk. The tree produces a lot of lemons, though they aren't very tasty, and they often grow in fascinating shapes. Have you ever seen a Buddha's hand fruit? They look like a hand, but with a bunch of strange and awkward-looking fingers. That's our lemon tree. Since the lemons are not great to use, they drop and rot on the driveway or front walk.

If my husband or I am not paying attention, one of us might hit our head on a low-hanging group of these fruits as we try to cut from the front door to the garage. When it rains, the lemons seem to hoard the rainwater until we walk under them, then dump the water down the back of our necks.

For all these reasons, we considered cutting it down on multiple different occasions. Then my husband started talking to the tree. He would say, "It's like that lemon tree is trying to get our attention. It grows the strangest fruit and drops it on us. It produces a huge amount of lemons, so we are always aware of it."

So, then the whole family joined in. "That lemon tree tries so hard. It keeps growing so many lemons. It's like it is telling us, 'Hey, I'm useful. Please don't cut me down. If I grow you cool-looking fruit, maybe you will keep me.'"

Of course, those were conversations we were just having with ourselves. We knew the lemon tree couldn't understand us, but something happened after we attributed these human qualities to it. After we started thinking of it as a living thing with feelings and needs, we couldn't cut it down. Now, even the thought of killing it feels wrong.

That got me thinking about the tendency humans have to personify all kinds of things. Personification is the act of giving human characteristics to non-human things. We all do this. We've always done this. If you're old enough, you remember Pet Rocks, right? We have given personalities and names to inanimate objects, such as boats or even the weather, throughout recorded time.

But in a world like today's, where loneliness is pervasive, personification becomes even more pronounced. Why do we do this? Why did my family so quickly turn an everyday tree into our friend, and how did that affect us? It comes down to the desire for connection. We're designed in such a way that we need to feel connected to the world around us, mentally, emotionally, and physically. For example, people pull over to watch a sunset or a wild animal. When I see something alive, I have this immense urge to touch it or pet it, and I don't think I'm alone in that. Well... maybe when I petted a bat in Bali, but he was so cute, and cuddled like a dog! I think I was just demonstrating our natural tendency to want a connection with the physical world. I don't believe that's by accident. When we run our fingers through a pet's fur, when we touch the physical ground, or when we breathe in the ocean air, oxytocin is released in our bodies. Oxytocin is the "love drug," so to speak. It makes us feel in touch and connected, which can calm us, make us feel more peaceful, and reduce stress or anxiety. Repeatedly engaging in such actions continues to trigger that release of oxytocin. That's why people live by the ocean or take up gardening. We're drawn to it.

That is markedly different from the connections we make with manmade things. The Human Improvement Project offers a quote that resonates. It says, "A new car might increase happiness a few minutes a day over a month or two. Even a new house only increases happiness a few minutes a day for a few months. For 99 percent of purchases, any effect on happiness lasts less than a few hours, yet people envy those who have nicer things and subconsciously assume they would be happier if they had those things." Those types of happiness do not last, whereas a pet, an ocean walk, or a beautiful sunset never loses its power.

We can even form a bond with something that doesn't exist yet. Do you remember wanting a pet as a child? You wanted it so bad that you could imagine the bond you would have with it, what you would do together, and how happy you would be. If you're a parent, you've likely experienced this in the context of having children. It is such a strong desire that our imagination creates a very real bond with something that doesn't yet exist. When it finally does exist, it's the most amazing sensation a human can experience.

I had always wanted children and often imagined what that would feel like. Although that experience came to me later in life, when I finally experienced that connection, it was overwhelming. When I feel overwhelmed—whether with bad things or good things—I write songs. So, I wrote a song called "It Was You." Being one of the first songs I ever wrote, it was recorded quite a while ago, but it hasn't been released yet. We filmed the music video in Vancouver, BC, at the beautiful UBC Chan Center.

"It Was You"

Use the QR code below to listen to "It Was You," an important song that was an outlet for me during an overwhelming time. I hope it will speak to you as well.

Having our daughter has been one of the most beautiful and grounding things in my life. It makes me think about things like connection, and makes me want to be the best person I can be in order to help *her* become the best person *she* can be. That connection gives me a reason and purpose. It makes me feel content and at peace.

When people are starved of real connection, they tend to create a connection of some kind. In the movie *Cast Away,* Tom Hanks found himself stranded on an island for years with no companionship. So, what did he do? He created Wilson. Wilson wasn't real. Tom Hanks' character knew that Wilson was just a volleyball with a face drawn on it. Even so, Tom Hanks' character became very attached to Wilson. He imbued that volleyball with a history, feelings, and thoughts, just like my family did with our lemon tree.

One of my husband's favorite books to read to our daughter is *A Coconut Named Bob,* which I've shared with you in a previous chapter. It's the story of a lonely little boy who finds a special coconut that becomes his friend. They do everything together, and the boy is horribly sad when the coconut washes out to sea one day.

The story picks up decades later, when the boy is a grandfather and finds his long-lost friend, Bob, on a deserted island. He walks up to what is now a beautiful, tall coconut tree, touches the trunk, and says, "Hello, Bob. How have you been?"

It's a children's story, but can't you imagine that happening? His connection to a coconut, which began when he was a child, followed him throughout his life. He was emotionally connected to it. I can see myself visiting our lemon tree in ten or twenty years and still feeling bonded with it. Isn't that remarkable? It's also healthy and pleasurable for me. I would feel all warm and fuzzy about that interaction, even though I know it is just something I've created in my own mind.

In an article, Matt Johnson, PhD, tells us something fascinating about Roombas. You know those little vacuum robots that run around? My family has some. We complain about them when it seems like they're lazy, or when they're noisily beeping at us like they want attention. We scold them when they come on during a conversation and tell them to go home.

I'm only telling you this because I now know our family is not unique. In the article, Matt Johnson states that 70 percent of Roomba owners give their Roombas names. Here is the most interesting thing: Roombas initially had a return policy that aimed to send back a working Roomba as quickly as possible, but owners pushed back against this. They didn't want a brand-new Roomba. They wanted *their* Roomba, even when that meant waiting longer or having it not function as well as a brand-new one.

There is no doubt in my mind that those people who sent their Roombas for repair knew they were robots, but they had formed a bond with them and saw them as more than robots.

The article continues this thought, highlighting how loneliness affects our tendency to connect with inanimate objects. Matt Johnson continues, "...when we're lonely and deprived of real human connection, we're even more prone to become attached to these inanimate entities." One would expect that, in a world growing more and more lonely, humans who are designed with the need for connection would try to connect in all kinds of ways. As I've discussed on the podcast multiple times, the promise of social media is exactly that. Marketers have discovered that loneliness is a market. They subtly promise a connection to something that will make us feel better, and we pursue it by the billions.

As already mentioned, a connection cannot be permanently fulfilled with manmade things. Whether a car, a house, or an app, these are all merely euphemisms for what we really crave—connection with the natural world and with each other. We will personify something to create a bond. It can be an animal, a Pet Rock, or a machine, but what we are really trying to do is to create something that connects with us. What we really want is a two-way connection. That's why we give these objects feelings and emotions. It allows us to imagine how they feel about us. We imagine they like us and need us, and that they are dependent on us.

When we personify something, we take care of it. When you personify a tree or your toaster, you take care of it. You handle it as if it were a person. You don't cut it down or throw it out. That bond creates connectedness that creates a relationship, which in turn teaches us something about the connection between humans.

If you ask someone, "How are you?" and get the pat answer, "Oh, I'm fine," is that a connection? It's an acknowledgement that you exist, but is that a true connection? How about when we have a talk with a friend over a cup of tea, laughing, telling stories, and giving hugs? Is that a connection?

It's almost as if everything in our world is reversed. We care about a tree, a robot, or a car. We treat them well, talk to them, and impute feelings to them. In my case, I'm willing to put myself in the tree's shoes—or roots, if you will—to imagine what the tree is feeling, even though it has no feelings at all. The living, breathing human beings we meet each day have emotions, feelings, and hurts, yet we hardly acknowledge that they exist. We don't imagine what they are going through. We don't even offer the smile or greeting we give our trees and robots. Because of that, as a community and as a culture, we have become detached from each other, making it easier to be rude, to hate, and to create enemies of people we have never even met. We don't see each other as humans. We see each other as less than the trees and household appliances we have befriended.

It hasn't always been that way in our communities. A hundred years ago, there were thousands of small communities bound by their connections to one another. If you look at nearly every human culture, they would spend time with each other, not just one day each week or month, but every day. They would talk, laugh, sing, and dance. They actually listened and expected a full response to the question, "How are you?"

In the modern era, there has been a lot of talk about "third places." This refers to spaces outside of work and home where people get together with the intent of creating lasting connections and being part of a community. It should be surprising that we have to be reminded to find these places, but in this day and age, people will pay for therapy and counseling that used to be available in our community.

Please do not misunderstand me. Therapists, counselors, and mental health professionals are very needed. I've benefited from them myself. What I am saying is that if we all had more connections with the people and the world around us, we would be less depressed, less anxious, more at peace, and happier. Isn't that the real goal in life?

There is something we can do today to help ourselves along that path, and it takes only a few seconds. We can give sincere smiles. We can be thankful and show gratitude to those around us—the grocery clerk, the garbage person, the receptionist, or barista. When we ask someone, "How are you?" we can pause, look them in the eye, and actually listen for an answer. Wouldn't that make for a better community and neighborhood?

Making a real connection starts with being honest. We can tell when someone gives us a fake smile or a fake laugh. Those don't carry any meaning or benefit, so let's try to be real. That doesn't mean we have to spend an hour sharing everything that happened to us in the last week. It does mean it's OK to say, "I'm struggling today," or "I'm having a tough day." It's also OK to say, "My day is going amazingly." Let's show our real selves and let others see who we are.

I think we will find that everyone has very similar feelings to ours, which will make us feel less alone and more part of a community. If you want to do something really special today, we can easily turn that fifteen-second action into something even more powerful. Ask someone else, "How are you?" Then add a "*Really*, how are you today?" Take fifteen seconds to listen. Do you think that would have an impact on that person today?

~~~~~~~~~~~~~~~~

In our interviews for this chapter, we asked people that question. One person we interviewed began by giving a good answer to the question "How are you?" They said they were very happy with their life. They commented that everyone has a mix of emotions in life; gratitude, happiness, and challenges are all part of the human experience.

They spoke about being more intentional about the questions they ask, picking up on where their last conversation with a person left off, and trying to reconnect on that topic. One example they gave was asking, "How is that project going?" as a follow-up from previous interactions. People respond better, since you're asking more specific
~~~~~~~~~~~~~~~~

questions—ones that matter to them personally.

You may have noticed that I sometimes share something I've recently read. Today, since we're talking about personification, I want to share a little story of my little bird friend in a different country.

A couple of weeks ago, we filmed the music video of my song "Could You Lend Me a Smile" in one of my favorite cities in Italy: Bologna. One day, I heard this beautiful bird singing outside my window. I opened the window to look for him, and I actually found him. He was a beautiful black bird sitting atop the building on an antenna. He was just sitting there singing, so I recorded his beautiful singing.

The next day, a friend visited me, so I told him about the little bird I had recorded and played it to him. As I played the recording of the bird singing, we heard another sound that was just like it. It turned out that the same bird heard his own singing and had come back.

I tried to imagine what he was singing about and what he thought he heard, and I wondered if I played the recording again, if he would come back. In the couple of days we stayed there, I played with this bird over and over again. I hope it was pleasant for him, but I definitely felt more connected to the city. I definitely want to go back for a visit and stay at the same apartment, just for my little bird friend.

Fifteen Seconds to Change Your World

I'm going to ask you, "How are you?" You can reply in your head or out loud. If that means saying, "I'm doing great," or if it means saying, "I'm struggling today," or "I need a hug," then that is the right answer.

It's the wrong answer to just say, "I'm fine."

Speaking of which, I saw a T-shirt that says "F-I-N-E." Below it, it explained the acronym: "F" equals "freaked out," "I" means "insecure," "N" refers to "neurotic," and "E" stands for "emotional." I think on many days that's true for most of us.

OK, here we go. "How are you?"

My Fifteen Seconds

I'm having a lot of fun doing the things I love, but I do feel I want to spend more time with my daughter. Tomorrow, I'm going to do better. I know she loves picnics, so that's what we will do.

Citations and references for this chapter are located at the end of the book.

Episode 10

Be Curious

I was watching a child during my walk today. She had to be about five years old. She was with her mother, who was busy trying to walk, but the little girl found everything so interesting, whether it was a ladybug or a dog's tail. They didn't get very far. I laughed a little too loudly to myself as I thought about how wonderful it was to be so curious. Being curious can not only help us rediscover our zest for life but can also save our relationships.

In pondering this subject, I began with one thought, refined that thought, and then refined it again and again. I went from thinking about active listening to thinking about showing validation to others, then to the importance of being interested in someone else. Finally, I arrived at the theme: Be curious.

Active listening, validation, showing personal interest, and being curious are all related. I was trying to accurately understand how one can keep a relationship—whether that's a marriage, a partnership, or a friendship—truly strong and healthy. That led me on a journey spanning several days.

So, we're going to go back a few days in time and talk about this meandering journey. I hope you enjoy, and more importantly, I hope you'll learn something about yourself. If you find yourself lost in the woods, so to speak, just skip to the end. Then again, the fun is in the journey, isn't it?

I started reading about active listening a while ago because I had read that phrase in some books. It sounded important, and as I'm always trying to improve my communication skills, I wanted to know how to do it. An active listener is supposed to give feedback that they're paying attention. So, for instance, if you say, "I was walking today, and a bird pooped on my head, ruining my hat," an active listener would say something like, "I'm sorry, a bird pooped on your head and ruined your hat."

Active listening is retelling what you've been told so the other person knows you're listening. I like to know when people are listening to what I say, and when someone rephrases it and repeats it back to me, it means they're listening to my words. They aren't just thinking about what they're going to make for dinner.

Both good therapists and good bosses practice active listening. Therapists can be great, and I've had a few good bosses, but when I'm talking to a friend, I like to hear something more than my own words repeated back to me. There is another listenin g method called validation. The definition I found defined validation as acknowledging and accepting another person's feelings and thoughts while showing that you understand their perspective and are listening.

Here's a real conversation I had with my husband after we left the

Monterey Bay Aquarium with our daughter recently. We've been there a lot, and it's always a special day. I asked, "What did you enjoy today about visiting the aquarium?" He answered, "I loved it because it reminds me how we were designed not just to live but to enjoy life. When you see those crazy sea otters playing, and the reactions of the people watching them, it says that we were made not just to exist but to experience happiness, laughter, and community."

I replied, "That's beautiful. I love it. I feel the same way." That's an example of validation. It is a step beyond active listening. I wasn't thinking about it at the time, but in hindsight, I was acknowledging his feelings. Then, I explained that I understood how he felt. Whatever it's called, it felt really good, and it was genuine.

Now, active listening would have been a little different. Instead of saying, "That's beautiful. I love it, and I feel the same way." I could have said, "So, you really enjoyed the sea otters and watching the people?" That would have acknowledged that I wasn't surfing on my phone while he was talking, but that I was actually listening to his answer. That's also good, but the active listening reply felt a little off, right? It was more like, "I'm acknowledging your words, but I'm not really invested in the emotions that you're having."

In a way, active listening doesn't require any real connection. After all, we can even feel someone understands us when we watch a video clip of them that resonates with us, and especially when they always seem to be extraordinarily good-looking. We feel like, "Wow, he gets me."

In hindsight, no, that person doesn't truly "get" me. He gets what he is saying, but that's a one-way connection, not two-way. If we're depending on those social media relationships to satisfy our need for human friendship, it won't work. That even applies to my podcast and this book. I'm grateful for it, and I feel like we are building something together here, which is why I really enjoy seeing your comments or reading your messages. It's also why I'm going to start doing some special interactive video podcasts. However, my podcast is not a replacement for having a close relationship with a dear friend who can look you in the eye and hold your hand as you share your deepest thoughts. That kind of relationship is really, really rare these days. So, if you have a friendship like that, you should nurture it. If you don't have that, and you yearn for it, that's what I'm trying to help us all understand how to create and maintain.

Active listening is good and serves a purpose, but I was on the hunt for the key to forming enduring, deep relationships that feel connected. Meaningful and active listening feels lacking. Validation seems to be on the right path. So, I started thinking about the relationships I have and asking myself whether the conversations I had with those people were building the bond I wanted.

I want to add something here, on a bit of a tangent, about the importance of those communication skills when things are not going well in a relationship. If we handle things well when things are going badly, it'll actually draw us closer to the other person. Validation and active listening are both necessary and critical when the other person has a problem with something we've done. In confrontational situations, our normal tendency is not to let the person finish speaking before we start with "But that's not true!" or another defensive phrase. With validation and active listening, we learn to put aside our immediate inclination to be defensive and instead concentrate on their feelings and words.

We can say, "I can see you are hurt," or "I can see that I hurt your feelings. When I left the dirty dishes in the sink, you felt upset." Those types of phrases are all practices of a healthy relationship. It helps us not turn things into even bigger issues.

Learning to validate a person during heated conversations has helped me immensely. The key to using active listening and validation during a confrontational situation is to pause. Pausing for a few seconds can change an outcome.

Take this conversation, for example. You walk through the door. Your significant other, without smiling, says, "You didn't do the laundry again. How come? Why is your laundry on the floor again?" You can feel the heat rising, like the little cartoon character with his face getting redder and redder until his head pops off. It feels like you have just been attacked. The temptation is to lash out.

What if you paused for a few seconds before replying, then used validation or active listening to give yourself time to take a different perspective? Note that we're using validation and active listening to buy time to remove our emotions. Then we also verbalize what the other person just said—something like, "I can see you're upset that I left the laundry on the floor." When we verbalize it, we give ourselves a chance to calm down, and we acknowledge the other person's feelings or words. I think the fallacy here is the idea that anger is stronger and that if we keep our cool, we are somehow weak.

In reality, what is harder, getting angry and losing control of the situation, or pausing for fifteen seconds to listen and reply with empathy? It's much harder to handle it the correct way.

Imagine you are watching these two people having that conversation. If the person who is being accused pauses and offers validation instead of blowing up, do you gain or lose respect for them? It's easier to give in to the anger. It takes a stronger person to pause, wait, and then answer in a way that diffuses the tension. It feels different in the moment, but the reality is that control takes a lot more strength.

I found that when I paused in a situation like this, it gave me a chance to think beyond the trigger to see what was important, and to see what I really wanted to happen. What I really wanted was a peaceful outcome. I got a lot of benefit from using active listening and validation.

Now, there are people I generally enjoy talking to, and others I struggle to talk to. Maybe it is just me, but when I run into one of the latter ones, it physically tires me out to talk to them. I was trying to figure out why I feel this way, and I realized that those who make me feel exhausted are those who are focused purely on what *they* are talking about.

Even when they asked me questions, I could tell they were just thinking about the next question or what they would say next. On the other hand, I think we all love talking to people who are genuinely interested in having a conversation that involves both of us. That's what I started pondering about.

Initially, I thought validation in conversations was the key, but I also wanted more than someone to validate how I felt. I mean, yes, it's nice when someone validates our feelings. Whether that means we're happy, sad, or something in between. However, having someone who is excited to hear what you have to say and who is on the same mental and emotional journey as you feels like a shared experience. It makes us feel good, like we have something worthwhile to say.

As I'm telling you all of this, some of you may be thinking, "I hope she never wants to be my friend. She thinks too much and is exhausting." I think my husband might agree with you, as I love having these deep conversations right when he wants to go to sleep. He would probably also tell you that I'm very shy around people and don't say much. That's true, but my mind is always going a mile a minute, which is why I think about stuff like this all the time.

Anyway, back on the subject. Remember, I'm on the hunt to find the key to building deep, lasting, and fulfilling connections.

In my prior relationships, there always came a time when I could feel the relationship drifting. Then I would wake up one day, wondering what happened to that spark. It wasn't that anything was specifically wrong. It's just like Barry Manilow says, "I'd lost that lovin' feeling." I apologize if you don't know who that is, but it was a good song. In previous episodes, you've learned that, like Mr. Manilow, when I feel a strong emotion, it comes out in music. The song I'm about to play is about the feeling in a relationship when everyday life has started pulling apart the bond you once had. It's that time in a relationship when nothing is really wrong, but you don't feel as connected as you did, and you aren't sure when that happened or why. It's called

"Falling Out of Us."

"Falling Out of Us"

Scan the QR code below to hear "Falling Out of Us" and experience my emotions surrounding losing connection in a relationship. As of publishing, this song is unreleased; however, most of my songs are available on my YouTube channel (MiistTheSinger).

It makes me sigh when I hear that song, but this chapter is all about how to avoid "falling out of us." How do we maintain a relationship so that we don't lose that special connection, especially with the people we deeply love? That's why I started pondering the need for active listening and validation, but as I continued on this journey, I decided it takes something more than both of those to really create and maintain a true bond.

I think we all want someone to listen and acknowledge our feelings, but it really makes us grow closer when that person is truly interested in what we have to say. When someone is truly interested in us, we feel that sincerity, and it gives us strength and confidence that we are being seen, heard, and that we are a valuable person worth listening to. That feels wonderful.

It doesn't necessarily mean the other person agrees with everything we're saying, but they get it. Even when they realize we might be experiencing consequences for a stupid thing we did, being truly interested in us, in essence, is saying, "They get it." They understand how we could do what we did. They love us still, and that makes us want to do better.

Being interested in someone also causes us to ask questions. When someone asks us about ourselves or how we feel, it feels good. That insight often changes our view of a situation or helps us see things from a different perspective.

There's a story about a woman on a subway whose kids were acting terribly. They were yelling, fighting, and bumping into people, but the woman just sat there staring at them. Many people were talking loudly about the kids and badmouthing the mom, until another woman sat down by her and simply asked, "Are you OK? Your children seem to be struggling."

The woman shook her head and said, "Oh, I'm sorry, I wasn't paying attention. We just left my husband's funeral, and I don't know what I'm going to do."

We've talked about validation and active listening, but in this case, those didn't help us. There was no conversation until someone was interested enough in her to ask if she was OK. You see, in that situation, there was no validation or active listening to be done. She didn't say anything, so the second woman had to remove her own initial feelings, put herself in that woman's place, and ask a simple question. Then she listened with her heart and mind. Being interested in that woman was transformative for everyone, including the widow, who didn't realize what her children were doing.

So, active listening, validation, and being interested. I know that is a lot to remember, so please stay with me, as we are going to make this really simple.

Being interested really applies to almost anything in life. It makes life so much more full. We see this a lot in relationships. Women are often attracted to men who are passionate about something. It doesn't even matter what it is. If a guy is really passionate about math, rocks, or their collection of nails—not toenails, the things you hammer into wood—the fact that a person is interested in something means that they might be just as interested in us. It might not work out that way, but being interested in something is attractive.

I thought of a family member who was interested in everything about everyone, to the point of being a busybody. They always wanted to know everything about everyone, and they weren't really trying to be close to anyone. I needed a better word to describe this act of building a bond between people, and my husband mentioned "be curious." I love that. Be curious.

When we're talking to someone, if we are truly curious about them, we will be actively listening. We will be validating and asking questions because we really want to know. That curiosity and the subsequent conversations cause a strong bond.

Being curious is attractive to everyone. Think about it. What do we like about young children? We have an expression that goes, "To see through the eyes of a child." That refers to how children are curious about everything, whether it's a bug, a bush, a bike, their sister's ponytail, or the dog's wagging tail. We are attracted to that curiosity. That means we feel a desire to connect with people who are curious because they're also curious about us.

There is a famous study about the power of asking questions and being curious about someone. The study showed that you can make someone fall in love with you by asking thirty-six questions. Whether or not they are actually in love is a question for another time, but the point is, really being curious about a person can and will create a lasting bond. That connection can last a lifetime and longer. If we find ourselves in a relationship that has lost that, perhaps it's because we have stopped being curious about each other.

I hope you enjoyed the meandering journey we took during this chapter. It took me a little while to get to the point here, but in actuality, it took me quite a few days to isolate what I was really looking for. I intend to be more curious now about our world, our community, you, and especially about those I love.

Fifteen Seconds to Change Your World

We're going to take fifteen seconds to first think of someone we want to be closer to. Secondly, we'll come up with a question to ask them. If it's a child, like my daughter, I might ask, "Why do you like unicorns so much?" or "Why do you try to trick us into thinking you've taken a shower when we know you haven't?" (I'm joking, but I would actually like to know the answer to that second question.)

If the person you chose is your partner, the question might be something like, "If you could do anything today, what would it be?" or "Where did you learn how to love?"

Whatever your question, it shouldn't have a simple "yes" or "no" answer. It has to be something that shows you really want to learn something new and significant about that person.

Citations and references for this chapter are located at the end of the book.

Episode 11

Why Do We Love?

I never went through the "Why?" stage when I was two years old. I think that's probably because my parents weren't around a lot, so I spent most of my days occupying myself. That's part of why I am grateful now that this gift of music has opened up so many different worlds to me. One of my biggest questions these days is: "Why?"

I don't know why God gave me this gift of music, but I want to use it properly, and I think the best way for me to do that is to be curious about everything. My curiosity creates emotions that come out in my music, allowing me to share my feelings and curiosity with others.

Science has offered many answers to the question "Why?" For instance, why do we eat and sleep? We know that if we don't eat, our body doesn't get enough nutrients, and we slowly die. If we don't sleep, our mind literally breaks. My daughter asked the other day, "Why do we put a lid on the frying pan when cooking?" Right as she said that, the salmon cooking in the pan popped, and the oil hit the lid so hard you could hear it. Question answered.

There are many studies on love, but shockingly few definitive answers. Even with a hundred definitions and theories about love, there is very little that science can empirically measure. Some people seem to have no capacity to love, but scientists aren't sure whether that's a genetic issue or a lack of nurturing in their lives. In contrast, some people love so much that their hearts literally break. It is called broken heart syndrome.

It's obvious that without love, our lives would be much, much different. It is estimated that 50 percent of all songs are about love, with over a hundred million songs written on the subject, and tens of thousands are added every day. That alone tells you there is a lot to say about the subject—it consumes us as humans. Thirty-three percent of mass-market paperback books are considered romance novels. Nearly every non-scientific book has an underlying theme of love: the pursuit of love, the endeavor to hold onto it, and the impact loss of love has on our daily lives.

We know we're capable of love; we yearn for it and revel in it. It can break our hearts, cause us unimaginable pain, or cause more euphoria than anything else in the human experience.

But why do we love? Why do we have this capacity? How does it benefit us, and is there a proper and improper way to love? That's what got me thinking this week.

Did you know that the Greeks had eight different words for love? Many languages, including English, have only one word to describe love. That in itself limits our ability to explain it properly. Think about this. We say, "I love this meal," then use the same word to say, "I love you, and I want to spend the rest of my life with you." Are those both the same kinds of love? Obviously not.

We can say, "I love my family," or "My best friend loves me," or "My neighbor loves my dog." We use one word for all those types of love. However, the Greeks decided to have different words so they could know what kind of love someone was talking about.

"Eros" is romantic love. That would be used when saying, "I love you" to a boyfriend, girlfriend, husband, or wife.

"Storge" is the love of family, the special love that means you can hate the person and simultaneously be willing to die for them. This word is where we get the idea of "family comes first," even though we may not like them very much.

"Philia" is something we, in the U.S., are familiar with—the city of Philadelphia is derived from this word. It means brotherly love. That's why Philadelphia is called "the city of brotherly love." This is the love of friends, including animals. So that bond you feel towards your best friend, or for Fido, that is philia.

"Agape" is the most used word for love in the Bible. It is a principled love. That means you can love someone you have never met. They're worth loving because they're a living, breathing, unique creature. Agape love is the kind of love that Mahatma Gandhi and Nelson Mandela called on to unite a nation of different people who didn't even know each other.

Then there is "ludus." This is a playful love, such as when you say you love baseball or love to sing, as I do.

"Pragma" is where we get the word pragmatic. It means a love based on duty or logic. In the days when someone would marry for duty, or for reasons other than romance, that was "pragma" love. It can also apply to a person who is a company man. He is loyal based on mutual benefit. He loves the company because the company takes care of him, and he works for them.

You've heard of the next one, "mania," which is obsessive love. When you hear of a stalker who claims to be in love with a person, that is mania. To that person, it feels like what they think love should feel like, but it's marked by insecurity and volatility.

And finally, there's "philautia." This is self-love, but it's broken into two parts: narcissism—love of self above all else—and normal self-love.

At the beginning of the chapter, you likely thought I was speaking of eros, the romantic love in books and movies between lovers. The question "why?" applies to all these kinds of love. Why do we love?

It's possible to live without the ability to feel or express love. Incredibly, it's estimated that this affects up to ten percent of the population. It is called alexithymia, or emotional blindness. People with this disorder can survive, but they suffer from depression, aggression, and suicidal ideation. Many people who suffer from this also came from abusive childhoods, showing that it can be a learned trait. Although they can survive without the ability to feel or show love, it's not a very rich existence, and it is depressing by definition.

On the contrary, we also know that people who love and are loved have much higher life satisfaction. They're happier, live longer, are more productive, and feel more fulfilled. Love also enables us to overlook others' flaws. If we love someone, we're more inclined to just say, "That's OK. I'll ignore that." It allows us to feel things more deeply, which motivates us to forgive those flaws.

Love enhances our creativity and imagination. When a person feels love, they write books or songs, then share them with the world. Someone can be depressed and write amazing words or create a powerful song, but someone who feels love creates magnificent art. When we love something, our hearts leap. We feel happy, and if a creative person feels that way, what they create is often spectacular. The Taj Mahal in India and the Eiffel Tower in Paris were dedicated to love. When something is so spectacular that it pulls on people's imagination, we often describe it as a labor of love.

Several studies have shown that love can slow your heart rate, lower your blood pressure, and relieve pain. One study showed that people who felt love thought foods tasted sweeter than people who tasted them while feeling jealousy. You would think that, based on how good it is for us, we're born knowing how to love properly. But is there a proper way? Yes, and that is coming from someone who learned the wrong way during childhood but is now learning the right way in my thirties. I can say definitively that it is so much better to experience love the way we were meant to. I'm sure this is how Italians feel about their pasta and how New Yorkers feel about their pizza. I'm kind of joking, but not really. If you asked the Italians and New Yorkers if there is a proper way to make and eat these foods, they would say yes. So, yes, there is a proper way to love.

How do we learn to love? Children learn by imitation. They not only imitate naturally, but they look for things to imitate. They'll actually stare at you, study what you're doing, then do the exact same thing to see how it works. They do that with mannerisms, speech, work ethic, and even cleanliness (though that last one is debatable when it comes to my daughter). They also imitate how we treat others and how we love.

If we, as parents, do not know how to love, express love, and receive love properly, our children will only know how to do what they have learned from us.

This manifested itself in my life in so many ways that it took me thirty years to learn what love actually should be like. That shocks me. It makes me sad, as well as determined to break that cycle with my daughter. I was raised never hearing "I love you" from my parents and getting beaten regularly to the point of bruises. I experienced yelling, screaming, and was finally abandoned at five years old at a boarding school. I had no idea how to love. I didn't know what it should feel like, let alone know how it was to be properly shown.

This is why an abused child often becomes an abuser or finds themselves in another abusive relationship when they become an adult. In some perverse way, they have learned that love and abuse are the same thing. The desire to feel love is an incredibly strong one. If the people who are supposed to love us beat us and scream at us, they're essentially teaching us that those actions are expressions of love. Yes, that feels wrong—my entire childhood felt wrong—but I had no other example to learn from. I watched movies displaying love, but you cannot learn how to show true love in a thirty-minute soap opera.

This kind of childhood results in a cycle of abuse that can run for generations and even affect entire cultures. Eventually, it can even become culturally unacceptable to say "I love you" between children and parents. How messed up is that? How is yelling at, screaming at, and hitting a child OK?

By now, you have learned that I use songwriting as a type of therapy. I wrote a song called "The Bruises Won't Ever Understand" about an adult who finds themselves in an abusive relationship because they were abused as a child. Now, decades later, they are finally realizing that love does not mean a closed hand.

As I'm writing this episode, I'm working on the scoring of this song. One of the key moments is when my six-year-old self joins me to express how this felt thirty years ago. It's painful but also healing to write this song: "The Bruises Won't Ever Understand."

"The Bruises Won't Ever Understand"

This is a heavy song, but I feel it's so important to our world. Take a listen, paying extra attention to the little girl's words at the end of the song. As always, to find my songs, you can go to my YouTube channel (MiistTheSinger) or search for them on any streaming platform.

At the end of the song, the little girl says, "You tell me you love me, but I don't. You tell me to feel, but my heart won't. You tell me that I would always feel your hand, but the bruises won't ever understand."

That is something that no child or adult should ever have to say. I hope my song will help people not only heal, but also help abusers see not only what they're doing, but also understand that their abusive behavior is not love. Abusive behavior is *never* love. In my case, my misunderstanding of what love is led me into a series of unhealthy relationships that were just as emotionally distant as my parents were. When that happens, you either slowly die or you find a way to convince yourself that you will be OK without fulfilling that desire for love. You shut down.

Remember that difficult word, "alexithymia," which means emotional blindness and the inability to feel or express love correctly? Repeated failure at love can lead to that.

Think of it this way: It's like each child is born with a blank canvas, meant to be painted with a beautiful picture of love, warmth, happiness, and joy. The canvas is meant to overflow with tenderness and acceptance; they're supposed to feel safe. The picture on that child's canvas is painted by their parents, and by the example they set. Once it's painted, that picture sticks with the child their entire life.

If that picture is one of pain, criticism, and abuse, that becomes the child's view of love. When they find themselves in a similar relationship as an adult, it feels so familiar that warning alarms don't go off in their minds or hearts. Of course, it isn't right. We know it's not right to be screamed at and emotionally tortured, but those of us from abusive childhoods are familiar with it, so we are attracted to that, and we end up right where we started. We aren't able to recognize what love really is because our parents didn't teach us that.

A few chapters ago, I talked about my song "She," a thank you to all mothers. In that song, I sing about the very special bond between a mother and her child. We call it the maternal bond, and it's one of the strongest bonds humans can form. While attempting to write the song in Chinese, I really struggled to express the idea of this maternal bond. It occurred to me that the Chinese language didn't have a word for it.

You may find that surprising, but it really isn't when you realize the history of the Chinese people. They have almost always struggled to survive, and having children was often more of a social contract. It was a way to be taken care of in one's old age, rather than being based purely on love. You have heard of the terrible genocide of baby girls. Tens of millions were killed or abandoned because society at large deemed them as less valuable. In a nation with limited resources, the "least valuable" are let go.

Mothers and fathers both did this. Chinese society deemed it normal. In addition, it was customary for parents to leave their babies with relatives at a very young age, then go to another city for work. Due to all this, the natural maternal bond was almost culturally erased. That's why there is no word for it. Think of what that has done to all the children in those homes. Most, like me, were never taught what love was. Not only were we never taught, but we actually lived the opposite.

Abandonment was common, as was a culture where you never told your child you loved them. Of course, China is not unique in teaching its children incorrectly. Every society has its own issues, and none of them do a very good job at teaching what love is.

If they taught love properly, our world would be very different. As adults, it becomes even more difficult to learn what love is and to unlearn what it is *not*. This is necessary for us to break the patterns so our children will find healthy, positive, and happy relationships that can help them bloom, prosper, and be fulfilled. The reward of achieving that is not just limited to our family—it affects our communities. It can change our culture and the world. Instead of living in a world without love, or a world that does not know how to show or receive love properly, we could learn to love the way we were meant to.

This is a goal that can only benefit us. There is literally no downside to learning how to love. As a thirty-something-year-old adult, I have now healed my relationship with my mother. I am very grateful for this. I recently learned to say "I love you" to her. It was very awkward at first, but now we say it to each other every night. From personal experience, I can tell you that this journey is worth it, but love is more than just *saying*, "I love you." That applies to our partners, family, friends, and everyone.

The words "I love you" are so commonly used that they sometimes lose their meaning. We can change that by thinking about why we love the person and verbalizing that specific reason. For instance, "I love you because you are always there when I need a shoulder to lean on or an ear to listen," or "I love you because you are the most kind-hearted child I could ever imagine."

Explaining why we love someone elevates the experience to something more powerful. That includes love for ourselves—not a narcissistic type of self-love, but a healthy and normal love. This is more than words of affirmation, but a truly, deeply felt truth. We should know why we love ourselves. It took me a long time to understand the need for this, as well as to overcome the embarrassment of even thinking about it. However, if we don't love ourselves, asking others to love us is essentially saying, "I'm not lovable, but I want you to love me anyway."

Why should someone love us if we feel that we are not worth loving? In Whitney Houston's song, "The Greatest Love of All," this is what she is saying. She's not talking about an arrogant or superior love, but a love that is necessary for us to feel worthy of the right to be loved. This is the right of every human on Earth. With children, if you tell them you love something, like their jokes, what will you get? A lot more jokes. If you tell them you love their drawings, the house will be filled with drawings.

It's the same thing with adults. If you tell them why you love them, they're much more likely to do more of that. This requires two things to work: one, us realizing why and how we feel loved. Secondly, it requires the other person to show us love in the way we feel it. This is the theory behind *The Five Love Languages* by Gary Chapman.

Just like a child learns to love from their parents, adults also must show their partners, friends, and children how to love them. Most of the time, it's done without much thought. We know that our friend

Jane loves tea, so we serve her tea. We know John always smiles when we hug him, so we give him a hug. Sometimes it takes a little more thought and attention. If we have a friend, child, or partner who tells us how they need to be loved, that is a very precious gift that we should take notice of.

For instance, our child often comes up to us and says, "I wish I had more hugs." It's awesome that they felt strong enough to tell us that. Now, it's up to us to provide it. If we repeatedly fail to do that, our child will likely feel they're not worth being loved because we, their parents, wouldn't give them what they needed. Adults are the same. If our partner buys us flowers and we respond very positively, we're telling them how we need to be loved. The other partner must then follow through with that, because if they don't, the requests will soon stop. When we feel like the people closest to us no longer love us, that leaves us pretty miserable, and resentment builds.

~~~~~~~~~~~~~~~

In our interviews for this episode, we asked someone if they say "I love you" often. This person said they don't say it very often, but think people should say it more. They commented on the fact that we can have love and respect for anyone, even strangers: "...if you have a big heart or any heart at all, we [should show] love [to] a lot of people." This person also commented that you might have to be the first to reach out and say, "I love you," for your friends and family to have the courage to say it back. I appreciated his candor.

~~~~~~~~~~~~~~~

After all is said and done, what is the answer to the question "Why do we love?" We love because it makes life amazing, and because when we feel we are loved, we create music and stories. We build, paint, and dance. We're more patient and kind, and we feel fulfilled, content, and happy.

Things literally taste better when you love. We're able to overcome problems more easily, we're healthier, and we feel less pain. A person who feels loved can see something beyond themselves because their biggest need is being fulfilled. If we see a world bigger than just themselves, then we have stronger families, better communities, and a more peaceful planet. Love connects us.

Everything about love is beneficial to us. We were made to love. We experience life to the fullest when we are allowed to feel it freely and express it sincerely. So, let's become love experts—not just for ourselves, but for everyone around us. What a remarkable difference that would make to our world.

This chapter is such an important one, and I hope you found a renewed sense of encouragement to show love and allow yourself to be loved.

Fifteen Seconds to Change Your World

This is probably the most difficult action I've asked you to do, but it is also the most powerful: To remind someone that you love them. It's best to do this in person, or at least by a phone call. A text really isn't the best way, but if you have no choice, do what you can.

It takes only a few seconds to call someone right now and say, "I just wanted to let you know that I love you. Have a good day." Imagine how that would affect that person. When was the last time someone called you just to say, "I love you"?

If you get voicemail, that's OK. Leave your message there. I bet they will keep that message for a long time. If you are feeling extra brave, add on why you love them. "I love you because you are the best mom I could have." And if you are alone today, look at yourself in the mirror and tell yourself, "I love you." That is a good place to start.

My Fifteen Seconds

I told my daughter that I love her. I said, "I love you, not because you are an amazing artist, amazing dancer, and a writer, but just because of who you are. I love you the same when you draw a beautiful picture as I do when you can't seem to do math. I love you even when you get in trouble, and it seems like I'm mad at you. My love for you doesn't change or go away because of the things you do or don't do."

I just realized I forgot to tell her that it's she and her dad who taught me how to love. I need to tell her that because it changed my life.

Citations and references for this chapter are located at the end of the book.

Episode 12

Humor: The Funny Subject

My daughter was sick for a few days. Even being sick, she was still happy and running around, but definitely in a bit of a fog. One morning at breakfast, she was half awake. I heard her having a conversation with my husband in the kitchen while he made her waffles to cheer her up. After pulling the waffle iron out, he sprayed it with oil, plugged it in, and closed it a little bit too loudly to let it heat up.

That got my daughter's attention. She already had all her waffle condiments out and a fork in her hand. She commented, concerned, "There is nothing in there." My husband replied quickly, "What do you mean? There's a very light and airy waffle. It's going to be really tasty."

"Oh, Dad, there is no waffle in there," she said in her teenager voice—and she's not even a teenager yet.

He said again, "It is a very special, light, and airy waffle. I'm sure if you don't want it, Dolce will."

Dolce, our dog, tentatively looked back and forth between them. This went on for several minutes, and I could hear the doubt start to creep into my daughter's voice. Either Dad was going crazy, or there was something wrong with her eyes. I found it very funny to listen to. In the end, she did get a real waffle, and Dolce got the imaginary one, along with a tiny bit of a real one.

A few minutes later, she showed up with a drawing of a little girl standing in front of a fridge. A cow was hanging out of the freezer, saying, "Help!" The caption read, "Mabel, take that cow out of the freezer, please. I hope you weren't planning on making ice cream." She obviously thought it was funny.

We find humor all around us. We watch funny videos of animals playing or of people unintentionally being humorous by doing something foolish, like jumping off a roof into a garbage can. We pay good money to see comedy shows, and when children discover things that make people laugh, it opens up a whole world of mischief. We even find humor in awful things, like watching cars slide down an icy hill and hit each other.

From a medical standpoint, humor is very good for us. It increases intake of air, improves circulation, and provides natural painkillers and stress relievers. Researchers have used brain scans to study the brains of people while they watched comedy clips with their friends. They found laughter increased pleasure and released endorphins into the brain. They also found that participants had a higher threshold of pain after watching comedy clips. I didn't ask how they discovered that.

The bottom line is, humor improves mental health, creating calmness and a sense of well-being. According to one study, laughing is also a workout. Even ten to fifteen minutes of laughter can burn up to forty calories. Maybe someone should start a comedy exercise club—they could call it Funny Fitness! Instead of personal trainers, there will be a lineup of comedians to keep us in stitches.

A giggle causes fifteen facial muscles to engage, resulting in all the funny faces we make when we're laughing. If something is *really* funny, our whole body gets involved. Our head, neck, arms, legs... and have you ever laughed so hard that your stomach hurts? Laughing is even an ab workout. The zygomaticus muscle—the name alone should make you smile because that is what it does—is responsible for the involuntary grin you have on your face when you're amused. The article warned that laughing too hard can unintentionally make you pee, so you might want to wear diapers if you're going to a really funny comedy show.

In 1979, Professor Rod Martin discovered that people who had a good sense of humor were less anxious and depressed. Laughter also reduces blood pressure. Studies have also shown that laughing at someone's joke is very important socially. People who laugh together bond and feel safer. It's an important way we connect to each other. When we hear someone laughing, we're more likely to join them. This is why we prefer to watch comedy with other people, and why Nate Bargatze sells out 20,000-seat stadiums.

Children learn this at a very young age when they figure out that making their parents or siblings laugh can actually get them out of trouble, earn them privileges, and gain more attention. If you have children, then you realize they may not understand what a joke is in the beginning. Our daughter accidentally made us laugh one day because her answer to "What comes out when it rains?" was "Reindeer."

For the next couple of weeks, we would get stories of random animals doing random things, but they definitely were not funny. However, since the reindeer joke got some laughs, she continued to make attempts, such as: "What comes out when it snows? Snow moose." These failed attempts at jokes and the subsequent attempts to explain what was funny were funnier than the jokes themselves.

We laugh at things because of the absence of logic. Think of a penguin wearing a tuxedo while dancing to show tunes—you get a movie *and* several sequels. Things in nature make us laugh because they seem to have an absence of logic as well, like a platypus, proboscis monkey, or a red-lipped batfish. Just looking at them will make you smile. Show them to a child, and they might just start laughing out loud. Someone had a sense of humor when making all the creatures around us.

Since songs and music are a big part of our lives, they can be humorous, as well. How about "Happy" by Pharrell Williams, or the song "Yes, We Have No Bananas"? Even the title makes you smile. "Dance Monkey" makes you want to dance and smile.

A while ago, I wrote a song about the things we all do when we have a big crush on someone, when we imagine what it would be like for them to fall for us. We know it's just a fantasy, but sometimes we ignore the logic and enjoy the daydreaming because it makes us happy. Growing up, it was too embarrassing to admit my fantasies to my friends. I knew how unrealistic it was to run off with my professor, but in my head, it was also kind of sweet. I felt it needed to be told in a song. It has a really cute music video, but neither the song nor the video has been released yet. It's called "If Love Were Just a Game."

<u>"If Love Were Just a Game"</u>

Experience the song here, along with the music video. I hope you love it as much as I do, and that it lets you experience a humorous moment today.

In the music video, I reenact a lot of these absurd notions. I think it's quite funny when I steal a four-foot-tall chess piece and run off. I know, absurd, but absurdity is a form of humor. In fact, there are over a dozen forms of humor. I'm going to attempt to explain some of them. Please forgive me in advance, as I'm not a comedian.

According to *Psychology Today*, if a man makes a woman laugh, that is a good indicator she is attracted to him. If a woman laughs at a man's jokes, even if they are bad jokes, it means she likes him. The more she laughs, the more she likes him. Men, however, do not experience the same thing with women who make them laugh, although men are attracted to women who laugh at their jokes. Am I the only one who thinks that is funny? OK, back to the forms of humor.

Number One: Self-effacing humor. This is when someone makes light of a bad situation. After spending eight hours making a magnificent cake, followed by a four-hour drive to deliver it, a very tired baker trips on his shoelace two feet from the table, and the cake crashes onto the ground. Instead of getting mad, he says, "Well, I'm going to be telling that story when I'm eighty years old."

Number Two: Self-deprecating humor. Imagine the same baker sitting beside the twelve-tier cake that was once a masterpiece. He reaches over, sticks his finger in a smashed piece, tastes it, and grimaces. He mutters, "Needed a little more butter."

Number Three: Wordplay. In the same scene, with the baker on the ground by the cake, a friendly man offers him a hand. He pulls the baker to his feet and exclaims, "Your cake was a smash!"

Number Four: Deadpan humor. The customer comes in, looks at the scene, and says, "You seem to have missed the table."

Number Five: Physical comedy. A child seizes the opportunity. He runs towards the fallen cake, trips, and lands headfirst in it. Instead of getting up, he just starts eating as fast as he can.

Number Six: Farcical humor. Seeing the child go headfirst into the cake, someone picks up a bit of frosting and throws it at someone. The person throws a piece back, and mayhem results with cake and frosting. The fight results in everything and everyone covered in goo. The dogs of the house come in and start licking everyone, causing screams, laughter, and more chaos.

Number Seven: Parody. A year later, someone throws another party where they reenact the cake-throwing fight, but with mashed potatoes, peas, and a dozen Vietnamese miniature pigs.

Number Eight: Observational humor. Jerry Seinfeld made this famous.

Number Nine: Surreal humor. Monty Python is known for this.

Number Ten: Dark humor. See if you can pick them all out in this story:

Have you noticed all the different kinds of emotional support animals lately? I get it. I wish I could bring my seventy-pound dog with me on the plane, too. I was trying to board a plane yesterday, and a man was attempting to bring a turkey vulture on as an emotional support animal. My first thought was, "Does he know something we don't?"

Upon seeing the turkey vulture, the flight attendant refused to allow him to board the plane, and the guy asked why. The flight attendant told him there was no room and that he would have to check the bird in. The man complained and said, "But that's not right. It's a carrion bird." (I'm sorry about that one, but my ten-year-old thought it was funny.)

The next passenger had a crow, and he was also stopped. The flight attendant told him that the FAA doesn't allow violence on aircraft.

The passenger, indignant, says, "What does that have to do with my crow?" The flight attendant calmly replied, "There are two crows onboard already, and three makes it a murder." (I hope you enjoyed that. Did you see there was wordplay in "carry on"?)

Number Eleven: Juvenile humor (bodily functions, mostly.) Why are kids obsessed with these kinds of jokes? My daughter just loves them. Maybe she will like this one: two turkey vultures are sitting on a telephone pole. One of them is trying to relieve himself, but is struggling. The other one says, "I told you not to eat that dead squirrel."

The reply: "I know; I have a really hard time passing them." (Take a moment to digest that one).

Number Twelve: Wit. This is a quick retort. It's what you wish you had said, but most often don't think of until hours later. Returning to the baker and the cake story, when the customer walked in to see this beautiful cake on the floor and said, "You seem to have missed the table." The baker could have said, "I thought we were doing a floor show."

Number Thirteen: Affiliative humor. This type of humor is centered on things that bring us together as a group or culture. Think of Jeff Foxworthy, or visiting New York and announcing to the crowd, "You gotta love New York. It's the only place where the rats have their own apartments, and you call them by name. Hey, there goes big Jim. Is that a Pomeranian he's carrying?"

Number Fourteen: Sarcasm. Nah... that's not humor.

Number Fifteen: Double entendres. Most of the time, people think of these as dirty jokes, but they don't have to be. Did you see the headline? Children make nutritious snacks.

Number Sixteen: Aggressive humor. This form of humor makes fun of other people. A comedian is on stage, and someone yells out, "You aren't very smart, are you?" The comedian yells back, "Well, you paid to come to see me, so what does that make you?"

There are others, but it took my husband two days to think of these, then he gave up. He said that jokes are no longer funny.

~~~~~~~~~~~~~~~

Have you ever seen someone pretend to laugh? It never sounds real. Why?

According to a BBC article, for something to be funny, we must find it funny involuntarily. In other words, we can't pretend it's funny. The limbic system of the brain triggers the physical reaction of laughter. The frontal lobe, at the very front of the brain, which determines our emotional responses, plays a part along with the limbic system. The frontal lobe is split into two halves, the left and the right. The left is the practical side and works out if the sounds and images we are experiencing are a joke or not. The right side is the creative half and determines if we actually find the situation funny or not. The frontal lobe cannot start our laughter, though. That's up to the limbic system, located beneath the cerebral cortex.

The limbic system handles basic emotions such as fear, anger, and
~~~~~~~~~~~~~~~

pleasure. Once it gets the message from the frontal lobe that we need to laugh at something, it sends another message, which sets the physical process of laughter.

What does that all mean? For us to find something funny, our brains must spontaneously interpret it as funny, resulting in laughter and movements in our faces and bodies. It also means it takes a lot of brain power to find humor in something, and that is why it is nearly impossible to do anything else. Try to hold onto a glass of liquid while laughing uncontrollably.

When something is very, very funny to us, we lose mental and physical control, even of our bladder. You've heard someone beg before, "Please stop making me laugh! I'm going to pee my pants." That's because our brains get so wound up in the humor that they have a hard time doing anything else. This is actually really good. If you are going through something difficult, or are sad or mad, a good laugh can help release that tension. You can't even stop it from happening.

The brain also floods the body with endorphins, which make us happy. According to the Nielsen Rating Company, we all have subconsciously figured this out because in difficult and uncertain times, people seek out comedy more often. It makes sense as it gives us a reprieve from the problems we face.

Humor does more than help us, according to *Psychology Today*. Those endorphins that the brain releases when we find something funny help us form bonds and feel connected to other people. Friendships are built because people feel better with a friend than without one, and laughter brings people together. It makes you feel good about both yourself and the person who caused you to laugh. As noted earlier, men who make women laugh are deemed very attractive. Why? Not only does it provide calmness and a sense of peace, but humor is seen as indicative of intelligence. According to *Psychology Today*, "Women view men who make them laugh as more intelligent than those who don't." Researchers speculate that constructing humor takes a high degree of intellectual power, especially when producing sophisticated humor. This explains why male comedians have such beautiful companions—have you noticed who Pete Davidson dates?

When women comment on what they like about their male counterparts, the answer is often "He's really funny" or "He makes me laugh." This shows the value that women in particular place on humor when it comes to relationships. I think, from a personal standpoint, having a good sense of humor helps us navigate difficult situations. I don't think I'm the only one to experience that. That same *Psychology Today* article went on to say:

Couples who share laughter experience more satisfying long-term relationships. Laughter keeps a relationship fresh and relieves the boredom that sometimes accompanies long-term relationships. In general, happy couples share more humorous moments than unhappy couples do. They also tend to provide a more enriching environment for their children, who tend to be happy and well-rounded. Humor can break tension in demanding situations...

When all is said and done, humor creates a connection between humans that is powerful, lasting, and healthy. Having a sense of humor will help us navigate through difficulty, weather our personal and global storms better, and help us resolve disputes. We don't need to stream a video or watch TV to find humor. We can see it in the world around us. Watch dogs or children at play. Take note of the birds and the beauty of a moment.

Look for humor around you today. Perhaps you will find yourself smiling or giggling a little inside, and that will enhance your daily life. Find humor wherever you are, and your life will be more connected and happier.

~~~~~~~~~~~~~~~

If you're like me, sometimes you get so busy that you forget to even eat, let alone take a break to de-stress. It feels like you never have enough time. No matter how crazy life is, we can take fifteen seconds. In those fifteen seconds, we can recenter. We've talked about taking fifteen seconds of gratitude, but we can also do that with humor.

Fifteen Seconds to Change Your World

Take fifteen seconds to intentionally notice or think of something that makes you smile. It could be the last joke you heard, maybe even one from my podcast. It could be a dog you saw, or that child driving his mom or dad crazy.

My Fifteen Seconds

There is a big window in our kitchen where our dog watches the delivery people coming into the courtyard to drop off things. She barks at them every time; she loves doing it. At night, when it's dark
~~~~~~~~~~~~~~~

outside and the lights are on inside, that window turns into a blurry mirror. So, every time we walk into the kitchen, she thinks she sees someone walking into our courtyard. So, she barks at them.

I imagine when she was made, she was given a choice: beauty or brain, and she was like, "Oh, 100 percent beauty. Brain? I don't know what that is. I don't think I need it." That could explain a lot of things.

Citations and references for this chapter are located at the end of the book.

Touch Me

I have a compulsion to touch. If I see the textured bark of a tree or a cute giant fruit bat, my fingers yearn to touch it. My mom says it started when I was a small child, when I discovered two bunnies at school. I was caught holding them by their ears more than once. Poor bunnies.

I think my compulsion started even before then. It started very, very young because I was left alone so much that my natural need to connect with my parents turned into the need to connect with *anything*. It didn't matter if it was a roly poly bug, the rough bark of a tree, the hollow but sturdy stem of a mushroom, or a delicate flower. I soon learned to connect to my world through touch.

A few months ago, my family and I visited an incredible zoo in Bali where there were all kinds of crazy animals, from big snakes to spiders the size of your hand. It was there that I met my first bat. He was about a foot tall, and the first thing he did after being handed to me was sniff my wrist. Then he licked me, nuzzled me, and cuddled my hand like a dog. I fell in love with that bat, but I was the only visitor who would touch it. That zoo visit was like heaven to me.

I have learned subconsciously that when things don't have a voice, they don't have a way to communicate with me, and I want to find a way to connect with them. I do that by touching them. When I do so, I get the tiniest of thrills, like a dose of love, so I keep doing it. Although I may be an extreme case, almost every child learns about their world by touching, whether that's grabbing the dog's ears or the nearest plant, or putting everything in their mouth.

Babies learn by touch as much as they learn by sight, and this is by design. Touching makes them feel connected to the world around them as they explore it. After all, what better way is there to get introduced to something new than to feel or taste it? That's what the bat did to me, and when he decided I was safe, he made himself at home in my arms.

Did you know that after a mother gives birth, the skin on their chest is one or two degrees warmer than the rest of their body? It creates a natural place for a newborn to feel safe. Mothers' bodies have the remarkable ability to regulate their temperature for the baby. If the baby is cold, the mother's body temperature rises. If the baby's temperature is too high, the mother's temperature cools. This shows that humans are literally made to feel connected through touch.

As we get older, it's not just any sense of touch that we find comforting. When we want to touch something, we do it in a very specific way. We don't walk up and hit it—although that would be a kind of touching. We don't grab it, squeeze it, or drop it. We use our fingers to stroke it, not too fast, and not too slow. The perfect speed is about 1.5 inches per second.

The nerves that feel what we're touching are called CT nerves. They're found all over our skin, except in the palms of our hands and the bottom of our feet. These nerves react especially to a light, moving touch that is about 89°F (32°C). This isn't a coincidence—that is the temperature of human skin. We immediately feel comforted by another human's touch. When touched the right way, it makes us feel close, loved, and safe.

We have all kinds of human touch: holding hands, leaning your head on someone's shoulder, hugging, playing footsie, walking arm in arm, spooning, or a kiss. Even saying each one of these phrases immediately invokes feelings. Actually doing them creates a special moment. Touch is supposed to draw us closer to each other.

I wrote a song about this feeling. It is called "Move Your Body Slowly." It is about the desire to be held and to slow dance with the one you love, especially when the rest of the world seems a little crazy. It's a fun song, not a serious one.

It has a fun music video, too, if you watch it on YouTube. It was filmed with the Golden Gate Bridge in the background at an incredible estate in Belvedere, California, with my friend Stefan.

"Move Your Body Slowly"

See my music video using the QR code below and hear the fun song that speaks of such a deep connection. You can find my music on other streaming services, as well.

Did you notice the line "intoxicate me with your touch"? That is, of course, what we're talking about here today—touch. Remarkably, we can actually feel intoxicated by someone's touch. Animals can get this way as well. Have you ever had a dog or a cat keep pushing or nudging your hand until you pet them? Do you find it hard to sleep unless a bit of your body is touching the one you love? Do your children come and snuggle you when you're just sitting alone? That is the compulsion to touch.

Sadly, culture has sometimes attempted to stop this natural need. Where I grew up, we never hugged. Showing any kind of affection, especially in public, was not acceptable. When the thought occurred to me recently, it made me quite sad that culture and family customs could stop such a basic human need.

Then I got to thinking about the subtle ways the need for contact crept back. In my case, although we didn't hug, it was acceptable to wash your children's or parents' faces. One of my fondest memories of my mom is when she would wash my face, and I cherished it. I remember it to this day, even though I don't remember being hugged.

Touch is such a basic need that when Michelangelo painted The Creation of Adam in the Sistine Chapel, he painted the finger of God symbolically touching Adam's finger. That makes sense, as the human finger is the most sensitive touch sensor known to exist. Our fingertips have around 2,500 receptors per square centimeter. Those 2,500 receptors each have their own function so that you can feel texture, sense temperature, wetness, vibration, pressure, and pain. It is specially tuned to feel a soft stroke that is the temperature of another person's skin. Touch is not just a capability that we have. It is something that enhances our ability to enjoy life in an incredible way.

Writer Lisa T. Lewis is quoted as saying, "Human touch is the most fundamental human need we all share, and we can't live well without it. We can survive, but we can't thrive." People who just survive are not very happy people.

An article by Healthline says that touch-starved people suffer from loneliness, depression, anxiety, high stress, low relationship satisfaction, lack of sleep, immune system disorders, and the inability to form healthy relationships. That is not a life I would want anyone to live intentionally. Sadly, this is the life that many are leading right now. It especially hurts me to hear about children who are living a life without physical connection, as that resonates with me personally.

Numerous studies have been done on the long-term damage a lack of touch can cause in children. Infants who are deprived of human touch, especially that of their parents, are known to have hyperactivity, aggression issues, trouble controlling their actions, and are subject to eating disorders. They isolate themselves, withdrawing mentally and emotionally. The harm goes beyond the emotional and mental harm. Children raised in orphanages without physical contact had stunted growth, abnormally high cortisol, and a high mortality rate. A study in the 1920s found that the brains of infants who lived without touch were 20 percent smaller than those who received regular cuddling and play, despite receiving the same nutrition and hygiene.

A lack of touch directly affects a child's likelihood of having a happy life. Skin-to-skin contact within the first few minutes of a baby's birth regulates their temperature, heart rate, breathing, and reduces crying. The benefits apply to the mother as well, with studies showing they are more relaxed, with an increase in oxytocin. It's as if we are hardwired to know this—the first thing a mother wants after birth is to hold her child against her chest. That mother-child bond is cemented right there, and the same goes for the father.

The importance of human touch, especially in infants, cannot be overemphasized. It is extremely important to the child's long-term happiness and their ability to pass on those learned traits to their own children.

In a study from 1965, a doctor named Harlow did a series of experiments on baby monkeys. Before I finish this story, his research is widely credited with causing the animal rights movements that we have today. I mention this because I'm going to compare those rights with the rights of human children.

In his experiment, Harlow created surrogate mothers made from wire and wool. In other words, intentionally not soft and cuddly. He also created another set of surrogate mothers made from soft, cuddly materials. The two surrogate mothers were placed in two attached chambers, but only the wire "mother" held the bottle with food.

Harlow found that the baby monkeys spent far more time snuggled against the soft mother than with the wire mother, even though the wire mother held the food. The conclusion was striking. We might need food to survive, but touch is what keeps us wanting to live.

Harlow's tests that forced baby monkeys to choose between survival and love were judged inhumane. But how many millions of people have to choose that life every day? Often, it seems we must create an impenetrable, hard emotional shell for survival. Otherwise, it seems we risk being seen as weak when showing our need for affection and touch.

That choice is an easy one for any infant to make in a literal heartbeat. It isn't even a question. The child would choose love and touch over putting on a tough face. We are drawn towards compassion, tenderness, and touch. Even if our culture or our own family does not display it, there are things we can do to help ourselves if we're in that situation.

Before I talk about that, I don't want to forget another huge segment of our population who are suffering because of this lack of touch and human connection. An article on Boundless makes the important point that neglected infants fail to thrive if they are not held often or given a lot of eye contact and verbal affirmations. Without those, they will likely experience social, developmental, health, and mental issues. This same problem occurs in our senior population, especially those in care homes. Loss of mobility and other issues can cause seniors to suffer greatly from a lack of physical contact.

The same article says caregivers should be trained for appropriate touch therapy as well as medical assistance. This can be as simple as placing their hand on a patient's shoulder or arm when talking to them, holding a handshake a bit longer, or giving a pat or rub on the back. "Such contact is vital for senior citizens, particularly if they are widowed, their families live far away, or visits are few and far between." Of course, all contact should be appropriate and with consent. However, physical contact is absolutely critical for us to feel human and connected with each other throughout our lives.

All of this is almost ironic, if it wasn't so sad. During the COVID pandemic, we were told to stop touching each other to save our lives—don't shake hands and don't hug. Be careful about being in close contact with anyone, even family members. While those instructions may have made sense because so many people were dying, think for a moment about the impact of three years of not touching. For three years, we lacked hugs, handshakes, and the warmth of sitting close to another person.

The lack of physical touch became an ailment of its own. New York-based psychologist Guy Winch, PhD, agrees: "Touch is something we associate with emotional closeness, and we associate the absence of it with emotional distance. We may not fully appreciate it, but in pre-pandemic life, there were literally dozens of small moments of touch throughout the day."

Today, loneliness is a worldwide pandemic, which no doubt increased during the COVID pandemic. Please don't get me wrong—I'm not making any kind of judgment about what the health professionals and governments did, or our actions as individuals. That is way above my pay grade and not my place to comment on. What I am talking about are the facts of what we went through: Three years of reduced or, in some cases, no physical touch. Everything we know about the necessity of touch would indicate that a world lacking physical touch would create widespread loneliness, depression, stress, and anxiety. I think that pretty much matches the headlines I see daily.

So, what can we do about this? Assuming we have consent, some things are obvious, such as hugs, holding hands, and patting someone on the back. But what can we do if we do not have those regularly available to us? Here are some ideas:

1. Go for a massage.

2. Spend time with animals. If you don't have animals yourself, go on a walk and ask to pet one.

3. Get your nails done. A mani-pedi is a great way for positive physical contact.

4. Get your hair done.

5. Learn to dance. I did a quick search around where we live and found over a dozen places to learn and participate in dance with or without a partner. There are likely many places around you that teach dance or have open dances. It's a great way to meet people, have some laughs, and connect with others.

6. Take a warm shower or bath. This one is interesting. Flowing water is as close as we can get to imitating human touch, and having a warm bath relaxes us as well.

7. There is one more option that I find intriguing, and in fact, I plan on doing it more. It is a known fact that gardening, putting our hands in the ground, touching plants, or being around the ocean, releases oxytocin (the love and bonding hormone that makes us feel connected).

Lately, there has been much writing about grounding. This is the idea that we should be physically connected to the earth at least once during the day. There is much speculation on this, but being connected to the ground or ocean makes us more relaxed and releases endorphins that calm and de-stress us.

So, I'm including gardening or being in or by the ocean on this list. We are designed to be connected with our planet, so it makes sense that the more connected we are to nature, the better we'll feel.

So what is our fifteen-second action today? We want to seek out the sensation of touch, but not just any touch. We want a hug, a handhold, or a shoulder to lean on—with proper consent, of course. Please don't hug a random person unless they agree to it.

I should mention the professional options. There are people you can hire to cuddle. From what I read online, some people have found this option beneficial. Before I met my husband, he was single for several years, and he said he would get professional massages regularly, which helped him feel connected. Whatever we choose to do, admitting that this is something we all need is important; we need to acknowledge it. Saying that we need human touch does not make us weak or needy, but it is a reminder that every person desires this most basic of human needs.

We also need to acknowledge that the human race lacks this more than ever, and we can change our world by being more aware and proactive in helping each other feel connected by human touch. Without regular human touch, we lose our claim to humanity itself. As mentioned before, children who are not given a loving touch have high concentrations of cortisol, the stress hormone. When that cortisol is not reduced, it creates high levels of anxiety, antisocial behavior, and often ends up in violence. The National Institute of Health reported that there is a disproportionate incidence of a lack of positive physical contact in violent individuals.

As children who suffer from this lack of positive physical contact grow into adolescence and adulthood, they display relationship problems, are more likely to use illicit drugs, do poorly in school, and are more likely to have depression. They also grow into less physically affectionate adults with more aggressive behaviors. This is sad, but it makes sense. The report states that the displayed physical violence is likely compensation for not receiving loving physical affection from their parents and peers.

Both their parents and peers affected how those children grew up. The bottom line is, we can all help this epidemic by the way we live our day-to-day lives. Showing affection and human contact is not a weakness; it's a strength, and makes us stronger and more able to overcome life's continuous adversities.

The study also talked about how to reduce physical violence and found that massage therapy was effective in treating violent adolescents. Why? Massage and physical touch reduce cortisol levels and increase dopamine and serotonin levels, resulting in a calmer, less anxious person.

Isn't it amazing what a little appropriate human touch can accomplish? Imagine what it could accomplish in our families and neighborhoods.

While our culture has both a positive and negative influence on fulfilling our need for touch, it really shouldn't. There is zero evidence that a child in France needs less touch than a child in the UK, the Middle East, Africa, or Asia.

The same goes for every adult. Every human on Earth needs human connection and touch. Saying that we don't hug in a certain culture doesn't mean it is less needed. In fact, it likely means that it is even *more* needed.

That being said, there are cultural and religious restrictions in many places that prohibit certain interactions between the sexes. Please don't get yourself hurt or in trouble, but find a way to give and receive the basic human necessity of touch and connection.

~~~~~~~~~~~~~~~

We all need connection. We need it with other humans and with nature. It inspires positive thinking and expands trust. It boosts our immune system, lowers blood pressure, increases calmness, and makes us feel loved. Connection is what makes us human, and being human means the need for touch.

Fun fact, in Chinese, there is a saying that literally means a long,
~~~~~~~~~~~~~~~

knee-to-knee conversation. It describes two people whose knees are very close or even touching while having a long heart-to-heart conversation. When we have a heart-to-heart conversation, touching the other person draws us closer, even if only our knees.

Fifteen Seconds to Change Your World

For our fifteen-second action in this chapter, seek out the sensation of touch—but not just any touch. We want the hug, the hand being held, the shoulder to lean on, with proper consent, of course. Please don't hug a random person unless they agree to it. You can also pet an animal, even a stuffed one.

If you're not somewhere where this is possible right now, please make a plan to do it sometime today. Review the list of suggestions we went over just a moment ago, and choose the one that you feel best doing.

My Fifteen Seconds

I went to pet my dog, Dolce. She was chewing on a huge bone, which is her favorite, but she surprised me by stopping for a moment to enjoy me petting her. It felt so good. Dogs are so special. Every time I pet a dog, the joy lasts for a long time.

There is something about the softness, the warmth, and how much they love it. They always seem so welcoming. It's like they're saying, "Yes, please. Here, here under my neck. Oh, under my armpit, too. Oh, don't forget my ears. Good human. You did a good job."

I'll pet dogs and any animals that allow me to touch them, over and over again; I can never get enough of it. (Sad note: On Dec 22, 2025, Dolce passed away. It has been a terrible adjustment learning to live without touching her. In her last few days, I was playing the piano when I saw her struggle to get up and come over to listen, which she often did. She would even put her head on my foot as I pressed the sustain pedal so she could be touching me. I say goodbye to her in Episode 39, "Three Days to Say Goodbye," where you will also find a special song called "Dolce's Lullaby. A Long, Long Dream.")

(Miist, with Dolce)

Citations and references for this chapter are located at the end of the book.

Episode 14

Living in Awe

Yesterday I was in my garden. In the corner, there is an old olive tree next to a tall wall. Together, they create an area of shade where a group of chubby baby mushrooms is growing. I find mushrooms so intriguing. They appear and disappear like ghosts. I found myself captivated by these little guys for quite some time. I felt as if I were a cloud passing over them, watching and observing them as they sprouted in their little community, a visitor to their little world for a few minutes. It made my day.

When I told my daughter this story, she reminded me of the previous summer when she had found green caterpillars on some leaves. We put them in an old, converted aquarium. Soon, the caterpillars made cocoons. After anxiously waiting for about ten days, we were mesmerized by the emergence of two gorgeous monarch butterflies. Watching that transformation was such a stunning experience, and like the mushrooms, it felt as if we had just been privy to something so intimate and special that we talked about it for weeks.

What we were experiencing was awe—not to be confused with "aww," the spontaneous cuteness response when seeing a baby… well, a baby, anything. For me, that experience is different in that we have a compulsion to grab it and cuddle whatever is causing the "aww."

Awe, on the other hand, is the feeling that we are privileged to see something, as visitors. It's a moment so special that it makes us feel special just being part of the experience. In that moment of time, it occurs to us that we are small in the grand scheme of things, in the best possible way. It's like there is a grand plan, and we have been shown a glimpse of the future and its possibilities. So we stand there transfixed, almost afraid to breathe, as if that would usher in the end of the moment we are experiencing.

A few years ago, my husband visited South Africa on safari, and after dark, everyone was supposed to meet an astronomer. In the middle of the night, they could hear all the voices in the tents as people got ready. As each group came out of their tents, they stopped talking until there was utter silence. This was because, as they exited the tent into the pitch dark, they walked into such an immense and vast carpet of stars that they couldn't speak. They didn't want to intrude upon the moment that they were experiencing. My husband said it was as if you had walked out of the tent right into the Milky Way and were suddenly in the middle of the universe, walking among the galaxies. It was a feeling close to sensing eternity itself.

We often find awe where we don't expect it. Dacher Keltner and Jonathan Haidt are leading experts in the study of awe. They have noted at least eight things that can make us feel awe: nature; music; design or art; moral excellence or altruism; collective effervescence or getting carried away by the emotion of being in a crowd; spiritual experiences; epiphanies—some people call this a eureka moment—

and finally, beginnings and endings, like birth and death.

Let's take a closer look at each one of those, as you and I may experience this differently. The idea today is to look for moments to experience. Why? There are many benefits to finding these moments, both to us and also because of how they transform our lives and our connections to others.

Nature. Probably the most common experience of awe is nature. My daughter's earliest recollection of awe is seeing tall trees all around her. She didn't remember exactly where or when, but it was somewhere around when she was two years old. My husband was carrying her through a forest of thirty-foot-tall bamboo in Hawaii, and her eyes opened wide as she stared up at the tall, swaying bamboo. She repeated, "Wow, wow, wow." To this day, she loves trees, and I think that was the day her love was awakened.

Music. Music is where I experience the most awe these days. As I've mentioned, I believe my gift of music came from God. That is the only explanation I have. I discovered it when I was thirty-four, and now, music just pours out of me. I have never studied music composition, yet when I listen to music, I hear not only the songs but the individual instruments, and I find myself writing compositions for some instruments I've never even touched. After those moments pass, I often feel as if I'm watching myself from far away and that person with this amazing gift is not me, but someone else I am amazed at.

I can't explain this gift or how the music comes out. It makes me feel like I am just a small part in a secret master plan I don't fully understand, and it makes me want to use my gift to be a part of a more important future.

Art. For many people, art is transformative. I didn't have that experience until about a year ago. My friend and famous drummer, Tim Alexander, has found a second calling as an abstract artist. Attending a gallery show of his, I tried to figure out what I was looking at. I asked him to explain it to me. He said, "Just keep looking at it until you see something." In about ten seconds, I could actually see a scene in the abstract art.

It was a street in Paris—music played, while people dined outside at cafés, but that scene was my mind's own interpretation of that abstract art. Every person who looked at the piece of art saw something different, and that blew my mind. For our brains to be able to see something that is only suggested by some flicks of the wrist, a brush, and globs of paint, that is awe for me. Of course, people get so moved that they spend their hard-earned money on art to hang on their walls because it brings awe into their lives every day.

Altruism. The LA fires in 2025 were horrible. Those first three days, people cried and held each other while entire neighborhoods burned. It was devastating to watch. However, about three days after the fires, people were doing amazing things. They shared, gave, and helped when they had nothing. Firemen and first responders worked unending days and nights to save a stranger's home or pets. Wedding rings in the rubble of a burned-down house symbolized the humanity in the disaster, bringing tears to many of our eyes. In this incredibly difficult and selfish world, people can still surprise and stun you with their selflessness, kindness, and compassion. I was in awe of them, as were so many others.

Collective effervescence. A month ago, I was invited to a Golden State Warriors game with the announcer, Franco Finn. I was greatly disappointed that Steph Curry was injured and couldn't play, but that is another story. There were 20,000 people there. There was a moment in the third quarter where the opposing team was two points away from tying the game, but a Warrior stole a pass, and a teammate hit a three-pointer. The stadium erupted. Strangers were high-fiving each other and jumping up and down. You could tell everyone had the same emotion—group awe.

Spiritual experiences. Many people have had life-altering religious experiences. Perhaps it is making a deal with God in a desperate situation. As the saying goes, "There are no atheists in foxholes." Others survive a drug overdose and wake up realizing they have a reason to live. Millions of people each year go on religious pilgrimages looking for these experiences. To some extent, festivals like Burning Man have also created experiences like these. Whether you call them spiritual or religious, people can feel in awe when they realize they are part of a bigger picture.

Epiphany. I find this one so ironically unexplainable. This is when someone thinks of a new idea. For instance, Alexander Graham Bell, who imagined the telephone, or Martin Cooper, the inventor of the first mobile telephone. Another example is Steve Jobs, who turned the mobile phone into the device we all carry in our pockets. Airplanes, driverless cars, rockets, solar panels, and the theory of relativity resulted from epiphanies, a brand-new idea that transforms the way people live or think, literally creating something from a thought.

The beginning of the universe and life is the ultimate something from nothing. As Carl Sagan was quoted, "If you wish to make an apple pie from scratch, you must first invent the universe."

Beginnings and endings. Women tend to experience awe more than men do. It's suggested that this is because of their emotional openness and social tenderness. They're often more in tune with feelings and things around them, especially other people. Women tend to be more connected to others, and nowhere is that more pronounced than in the birth of children. The entire process can be full of awe, from creating a new human life within her body to watching that new life become its own person. It can deeply affect a woman's life. To me, there is nothing more miraculous than the creation of a new life with an individuality that has never existed before and will never exist again.

~~~~~~~~~~~~~~~

Awe is not always a purely positive emotion. When staring down the precipice of the Grand Canyon or from the top of a tall building, we can be in awe of the amazing feast to our eyes as well as fear, knowing that a false step could cost us our lives. It could be on a hike in the wilderness, then stumbling upon a grizzly bear, making your heart stop, but incredibly moving all at the same time.

Experiencing death can cause awe in many ways. Dr. Andy Tix commented, "I have led courses in the psychology of the Holocaust, for instance, including trips to Holocaust sites in Europe, and rarely have I seen students so absorbed or affected by phenomena being studied as when we directly encountered the overwhelming memorials of death we visited." Of course, often, when seeing a person
~~~~~~~~~~~~~~~

pass away, we are struck by our own mortality and smallness in the universe. That causes us to wonder and contemplate our purpose. What happens after that is awe.

Other things that can cause awe, even achievements of our own or others, can result in awe, to some extent. However, these are the main eight ways that humans experience awe, which permeate our lives and daily moments.

For me, there have not been enough moments of awe. I'm always looking for them. After getting married, I'm now raising my stepdaughter. I am in awe of the person she has become and the person that I have become as her mother. I love that she, without hesitation, calls me "Mom." I wrote her a song, called "It Was You," dedicated to the awe of my daughter and our relationship.

"It Was You"

When I play this song for people, they listen to it as if it were a love song. It is, but it doesn't fully occur to them who the love song is about until the sound of the baby at the end. That is an actual recording of my daughter cooing when she was a baby. When those with children hear that cooing, I often see smiles and nodding heads.

Awe has so many benefits for me; it reminds me what an incredible gift it is to be alive. Our bodies are so incredibly designed not just to live but to enjoy both the smallest and biggest of moments. If we choose to, we can find wonder in a ladybug, at Niagara Falls, or in the dunes of the Sahara. We can find it by looking into the eyes of our children, or watching a hummingbird hop from flower to flower. Our lives are filled with opportunities to feel awe. When we do that, our stresses and problems come into perspective. Experiencing awe is scientifically shown to reduce stress and anxiety. It increases creativity, helping us learn and see things in a different light. That is why artists, musicians, and creative people use those moments of awe to inspire themselves to create or think beyond the boundaries of everyday limits. It pushes us to find, explore, and increase our knowledge as well as to connect more with the world around us. By doing so, it increases our social connections because we are compelled to share these moments with others. It also makes us more compassionate as we contemplate how small we are and that, in the end, there is nothing more fulfilling than helping others.

The golden rule is, in fact, the best way to live: simply treat others as you want to be treated. That means reaching out to help, showing empathy, and offering a shoulder to cry on when needed. When we do all these things, our lives are filled with meaning and purpose, which benefits us mentally, physically, emotionally, and spiritually.

Awe is truly inspiring, and there is science to back it up. There is a Default Mode Network, also known as DMN. It is a system within our brain that lights up when we're not completely focused on what is around us, when we are trying to be empathetic and understand where another person is coming from, or when reminiscing about the past and pondering our future. When we do those things, our focus is not on the immediate here and now. This DMN kicks in, becoming more active. You would think that happens when we feel awe, but it is actually the opposite. When we feel awe, the DMN becomes less active, not more.

Psychology Today explains that the DMN is the part of the brain associated with self-referential thinking, our constant inner monologue about ourselves, our worries, and our plans. By quieting this network, awe allows us to feel less self-focused and more connected to the world around us. In other words, by quieting the DMN, we feel more connected to the universe and less connected to ourselves, our thoughts, and our past or future. It instead allows us to be part of a much bigger picture, which explains why a common result of awe is the feeling that we are small in the face of whatever we witness.

Awe engages the prefrontal cortex as well. That part of our brain helps us understand complex ideas and abstract thoughts. We are more open to experiences we have not previously had. For instance, we may have never wanted children, but may find ourselves faced with the immediate and real possibility of never having one. Perhaps a doctor suddenly recommends a hysterectomy—remember, awe can involve fear. With this shocking news, we find ourselves in awe, and all of a sudden, contemplating what it might be like to have a child.

Such moments of awe can be life-altering from a purely physical measurement. Being in awe releases oxytocin, the love hormone. This hormone connects and bonds us with others.

In Maui, we see this almost nightly at sunset. All the locals and tourists, who sometimes do not get along, go to the ocean to watch the sunset. There can be hundreds of people there in those final moments of the day. When the sun dips to the horizon, the water lights up and dances, then the sun drops behind the wall of water. The sky lights up in spectacular colors of fire, and everyone is silent. Everyone is holding hands or leaning on each other.

When it is finished, there is a connection with everyone there. It is as if we all shared a special, secret moment that has drawn us together. Awe often includes a tenable feeling of connection with those around us. If that weren't enough, awe has also been shown to be anti-inflammatory, reducing stress, and making us healthier.

What does this all tell us? We should be experiencing more awe in our lives because it alters us in a positive way. We can do that intentionally. In an article by Eben Harrell in the *Harvard Business Review*, she cited an experiment. Visitors to a scenic overlook at Yosemite National Park who were asked to draw it consistently made themselves smaller in their pictures than visitors in downtown San Francisco did, suggesting a diminished sense of self-importance while physically in nature.

In another experiment, volunteers who were told to gaze at enormous eucalyptus trees were asked to be paid less for their participation in the experiment than those who were told to stare at an academic building. In other words, we prefer to look at nature rather than something man-made because it triggers in us an oxytocin response. The first volunteers were also more willing to help pick up pens dropped by a study organizer while in nature. Awe actually alters the way we see ourselves and makes us more willing to help, benefiting others, but it also makes us feel good. It's like we were designed that way.

Awe is not just something for children. It is for every one of us. It is a reminder of what it means to be curious, aware, and appreciative every day of our lives. It is a way of seeing and living—a way to be. It heals us, encourages us, makes us feel alive, and connects us with others.

Find something to be in awe of every day. You and I are surrounded by reasons to be in awe. We just need to look for them.

Use the eyes of a six-year-old child when you see a flower breaking through a concrete wall. Find the wonder in that. When you walk out at night and see a star that likely existed thousands of years ago, ponder what that means. When you look into the faces of your children and see your eyes and nose and that freckle, marvel at how incredible that is. Perhaps in these moments of awe, we will find ourselves as we once were and the person we long to be.

Fifteen Seconds to Change Your World

This one will seem so simple, but it's not. It likely requires us to do something we're out of practice at—find awe in something. Look around you. What do you see? Do you see people or animals?

Are you driving, and you see lots of things happening? Try to look at the things around you as if you were a newborn baby, observing them for the first time. Do you see a puppy, a tall tree, people holding hands, or a person eating something? Whatever it is, stop and ponder how amazing it is. Even something as common as eating. Think about the human ability to taste food and feel texture. Think about how happy food makes us, and why it does that. Why doesn't everything taste like oatmeal? I don't hate oatmeal, but I'm glad a chocolate donut doesn't taste like it. What an amazing gift. Do we appreciate it?

Do you see that tree? How does it grow so tall and stand through all those storms and droughts? Think of all the animals and creatures that call it home and the peacefulness it brings.

If you're typing on a keyboard, how can you do that and listen to me at the same time? Aren't your fingers and hands incredible tools? They can build a home as well as tenderly touch the face of someone you love.

You see, there is awe all around us. We just have to learn to see it again.

My Fifteen Seconds

I'm holding a shell. I don't know the actual term for it, but it was the outside layer of what used to be a chrysalis. We, as a family, watched another caterpillar transform into a butterfly this year because we enjoyed the experience so much last year. I'm in awe every time I see a butterfly. That's what I did for my fifteen seconds.

Citations and references for this chapter are located at the end of the book.

Episode 15

I Know You Think You Heard What You Think I Said, but I'm Not Sure That You Realize That What You Heard is Not What I Meant

I know you think you understand what you think I said, but I'm not sure you realize that what you heard is not what I meant." I love this quote by Robert McCloskey because it unclearly states the obvious—communication can be complicated.

Around 5:00 p.m. every day, my dog somehow knows it's dinner time. She starts dancing around, running back and forth from her food container to us. We obviously know what she wants, but we always pretend we're confused. She then touches the container with her nose and looks toward her bowl. If we still don't react, she jogs in place, all four legs moving, until we open the food container and give her dinner.

She is communicating quite well, but gets frustrated when we pretend we don't understand. Have you ever felt that way? You try to tell someone what you need or want, and they just don't get it.

There is the old story about the wife who laments, "I wish the house were cleaner." The next day, the husband brings home a new vacuum cleaner and presents it to her, expecting gratitude and happiness, but is surprised when he gets the opposite.

There are entire books on the subject of communication between the sexes. John Gray's *Men Are from Mars, Women Are from Venus* has sold over fifty million copies and has been translated into fifty languages. That tells you how prevalent miscommunication is, and that is just between partners.

Most of the time, miscommunication is merely an inconvenience and downright funny. Have you ever had a bad autocorrect? My husband thinks Siri has a dirty mind because she's always misunderstanding him and adding swear words to his messages. In over ten years, Siri hasn't figured out that he doesn't use swear words.

Autocorrects are usually just comedy fodder. I loved the following thread between two friends.

Friend One: You would not believe the day I had. I devoured a baby in a cab.
Friend Two: YOU WHAT?
Friend One: Oh, God, "delivered." Oh, this phone...
Friend Two: OMG, wow, boy or girl?
Friend One: Gorilla.
Friend One: GIRL.

Technology is supposed to help us communicate better, but that is often not the case. This other person asked Siri, "I think I have alcohol poisoning. What do I do?" Siri replied, "I found seven liquor stores fairly close to you." Not a great response.

Miscommunication happens between friends, neighbors, companies, and even countries every minute of every day. It is such a challenge to communicate between countries that we have an entire group of people called diplomats who are deemed necessary to explain, interpret, and help avoid disastrous miscommunications.

Thinking that everyone should think the same way we do is not only unrealistic but also dangerous. In a very real sense, wars have been started over words that were taken the wrong way. Nuclear war has almost happened several times because words were not taken as expected.

Science is supposed to be measured by strict rules, but in a spectacular failure to communicate, a NASA team on Earth lost communication with the Mars Climate Orbiter soon after launch. The computer on the ground was using the standard system of time, while the one on the spacecraft used the matrix system. The spacecraft fell apart upon entering Mars' orbit.

Of course, most of the time we are not dealing with nuclear war or spacecraft, but rather communication between people. While miscommunication can sometimes be funny, many times it causes serious challenges.

I like this quote from Amy Tan in *The Joy Luck Club*: "My mother and I never really understood each other. We translated each other's meaning, and I seemed to hear less than what was said, while my mother heard more." Those are two people who spent decades together and couldn't figure out how to communicate. Many of us have lived that, but how is that possible when two people are actually trying to communicate? Why can't they understand each other?

In that story, the mother and daughter both wanted to be heard and understood. There was no hatred or malice between them, but they each couldn't find a way to see where the other was coming from. That resulted in a disconnection in a relationship they both desperately wanted and needed. In the end, that is what communication is supposed to do for humans. Connect us.

Animals communicate, too, most often for practical reasons like food, mating, and danger. Humans communicate for all those reasons, but more importantly, to feel close and connected, and to make plans. They also talk about the past and contemplate their futures. How many marriages end in divorce because they find themselves drifting apart with different goals, desires, and lives? This is a huge cause of divorces—lack of proper communication.

My relationships followed a pretty standard pattern. We were happy, then we communicated less and less until we completely stopped talking. Then the relationship fell apart. For other friends of mine, it was a little different. They communicated constantly, just not nicely. They argued and talked at each other constantly, but could no longer understand each other. I don't know which path is worse, but the result is the same.

"Tell Me What You See"

One of my songs, "Tell Me What You See," is about failure to communicate. It is when one person in a relationship becomes emotionally distant, and the other is searching for the reason why, but is left only with questions. I think you will be able to relate to how painful this feels.

If you have ever felt that way, you know how a lack of communication can make you feel hollow and like you are drifting without direction. Remembering that feeling drove me to write this episode. Almost anyone who has been in a long-term relationship has asked this question either out loud or to themselves, and it's the lack of an answer, the lack of knowing, that causes the most pain. Most of the time, that pain is not caused intentionally. It is because of the other person's inability to explain where they're at, what they need or want, and what that means to them and to their partner.

So why do we fail so badly in communication? There are five or six main reasons our communication is failing that we can pinpoint, and by identifying them, we can learn to improve it and maintain our relationships without so much pain and misunderstanding.

Women, more than men, measure themselves by the strength of their relationships. If a woman doesn't have close relationships, especially with her family, she is more likely to identify herself as a failure. That doesn't mean men don't value relationships highly, but they often measure their self-worth by their work. That, too, is heavily impacted by their ability to communicate. No matter who we are, the ability to communicate well will affect us for our entire lives.

In communication, the first thing we must understand is that we communicate from our personal perspective, from inside our mind, heart, and where we are in our lives at that moment. That is a crucial point to remember. Our personal bias, culture, present emotions, and beliefs all impact how we communicate.

For instance, the woman who says to her husband, "I wish the house were cleaner," might be overwhelmed, frustrated, and exhausted. That statement was also molded by the way she learned to communicate as a child. It is not a direct statement: "I wish you would help me keep the house cleaner by wiping your feet." In fact, the way she said it could be taken as either a statement or a complaint.

Her beliefs also come into play. Perhaps she grew up feeling that everyone should contribute to the housework, whereas her husband grew up in a more traditional household. Do you see how this situation is developing?

Lastly, perhaps she is from a culture where people remove their shoes, and while she understands her husband is not from the same culture, that belief could cause deep-seated frustration. The woman's perspective is completely molded not only by the words, but also by the expectations of what she said.

Let's take a look from the husband's perspective. He heard, "I wish the house were cleaner," as a problem that needed to be solved. Since he grew up in a traditional household, it never occurred to him that his wife might have meant she wanted him to help with the cleaning.

His emotional state could have been happy, and his cultural background backed him up. "Oh, I know what I can do to help my wife!" He decides to make what he saw as his wife's job easier.

I'm not getting into who was right and wrong because very likely neither was. The key to remember when dealing with male-female communication comes from Emerson Eggerichs, the bestselling author of *Love and Respect*. He asserts that women need love, and men need respect, which is both simple and complicated. If you are talking to a woman, lead with love. If you're talking to a man, find a way to give him respect. To communicate and expect to be understood requires us to realize that what and how we say it begins with a bias. Our own bias.

To communicate accurately requires that we say more than words. We have to convey it in a way that the other person clearly understands what we are saying and what our expectations are. To do that, we have to understand where the other person is figuratively sitting at the moment.

On the other side, the listener must also be able to listen from the other person's perspective. If this sounds ridiculously difficult and you're ready to throw up your hands, that is why we so often fail at communication. I assure you, there is a simple key that will help us all communicate better. Just hang on for a while longer.

To summarize, our attempts to communicate with another human are impacted by multiple things. Our thoughts, before we even speak, are shaped by our own knowledge, emotions, and expectations.

The words we choose usually do not fully convey our intended message. We expect mind-reading much of the time, which is inherently unfair. The listener perceives the words based on their own experiences and understanding. The interpretation of the listener may differ from the speaker's intent. The original message could be lost or altered due to both parties' bias.

Think of these steps in the context of my dog asking for dinner.

Step one: The dog is thinking, "I'm hungry."

Step two: The dog is dancing around, pointing at the food. "Obviously, the human should understand."

Step three: "The human is not hearing what I'm saying."

Step four: "Why is the human talking to me instead of giving me food?"

Step five: "I think the human is stupid."

I know it's funny, but how many times have we had a conversation that ended up with step five? "I think that person must be stupid because they don't understand." Only, with another human, it is not so funny.

In *The Joy Luck Club,* the conversation between the mother and the daughter had very strong cultural issues. The mother had been raised in China, and the child in the U.S.

From personal experience, I know this creates a big gap in understanding and implication. For instance, in China, it is acceptable to just tell someone they look fat. In fact, sometimes that is taken as a compliment, but if you say that to someone in the Western world, you would be viewed as rude. In Japan, silence in conversation is polite, while in America, silence is awkward.

Many words or concepts cannot be directly translated from one language to another. In one language from Africa, there is no direct translation of the word for "perfect." The closest thing is a ripe peach.

In what is commonly known as the "Thee Our Father" prayer, in English, we pray for God to give us our daily bread, but if you translate that directly into Chinese, the meaning would be very different. The word for bread in Chinese translation is a flat, pancake-like dough. Western bread would be viewed as being eaten by wealthy people, which would change the entire meaning of the prayer.

Some concepts cannot be easily translated either. In a prior chapter, I talked about how the Greeks have eight words for love. We have one in English. Also in English, we use the word "azure" to mean a color of blue. To those in Portugal, it means much more—that is, the color of their sky, their ocean, and their life.

In China, what we would call black tea is called red tea. Many other cultures have beautiful words, which I cannot pronounce, for concepts that we really should have words for.

"Wabi-sabi" is a Japanese word that describes the beauty of imperfection. **"Saudade"** is a Portuguese word that describes the longing for someone or something that is gone, and **"Sobremesa"** is a Spanish word that describes the time spent at the table after a meal.

"Verschlimmbessern" in German means to make something worse while trying to improve it. One of my favorites is **"iktsuarpok,"** an Inuit word that captures the feeling of anticipation when waiting for someone to arrive. There is even a German word describing a face that badly needs a punch: **"backpfeifengesicht."** I'm not sure what that says about the German culture, but I found it interesting that they felt the need to create a word for this. You can start to see how cultural differences can cause big problems in communication.

Then there are the generational differences. For a forty-year-old, receiving a message without proper punctuation and capitalization can be seen as lazy and rude, while to a Gen Zer, it is perfectly acceptable.

Studies have shown that many Gen Zers are anxious about taking phone calls and would rather communicate through text, while Gen Xers and Boomers prefer phone calls. In fact, sending a text for a sensitive subject could be considered rude by those generations. Trying to communicate is confusing, to say the least.

I'm thirty-seven, so I'm right in between generations, and I'm so confused. I don't know what I prefer, but if I had to choose, I would say, "Text me first, then talk on the phone."

Another one, of course, is the political divide that is so deeply rooted these days. People are so divided that they literally express hatred towards others whom they have never met, but who do not share their views. While there have always been opposing views, it seems the chasm has grown so wide that people do not even see the opposing side as human anymore. You can simply observe the world today and see what that results in.

Quite a bit of research suggests that this widening gulf of communication is also due to data-driven algorithms that reinforce our personal biases and beliefs. In other words, the tech companies know so much about us from our digital activities that almost everything we see online is what we already agree with. They do not readily share opposing views because we don't like them, but that only encourages and feeds a loop of communication that excludes those who do not believe what we do. The division becomes greater and greater because it is a self-fulfilling loop that can only make communication more difficult—and it was hard to begin with.

How did we get to this point? We are the most wired yet disconnected generation to live. As humans, we need not only to be physically connected to each other and the Earth, but we also need to feel connected. If we do not feel connected, science has shown that it gives rise to anxiety, fear, and stress, which makes communication more difficult.

Our modern types of communication make it harder for past generations. Humans were meant to communicate face-to-face, but now we text, we're on social media, sending DMs, likes, and messages. We sit in on Zoom meetings and communicate remotely. We have forgotten that 55 percent of communication is nonverbal. Think about that. We have a hard enough time communicating with people who are literally in front of us. Now, take away over half of our ability to communicate when we meet remotely by text, DM, or video calls.

Imagine having a serious conversation with your child in person. Now take away half of your words. Instead of, "I want to talk to you about how you have been treating your brother," you say, "I to you about have been brother," and then expect your child to understand and react appropriately.

Who in their right mind would expect a child to understand and react appropriately when they can only hear half of your words? That is, in essence, what our expectations are. When we have serious conversations by text or even by video, we miss over half of the nonverbal communication. We may not realize that silence is embarrassment, shame, or pondering, and instead we interpret it as arrogance, distraction, or uncaring.

That is, in reality, what can easily happen and has happened. I'm sure I'm not the only one who has sent a text that's been misinterpreted by the receiver. Yesterday, I did this in person, face-to-face. I was washing my hands in my mom's bathroom, and there was no towel. My mom told me multiple times she was washing the towel, so there was no towel. Without thinking, I said, "Yes, Mom, you have told me three times that you are washing your towels."

She looked hurt. It took me a while to think about it. You see, her mother died a few months ago. My mom took care of her day and night, and during that time, my relatives would complain because my grandmother would repeat the same things over and over again and immediately forget them. By me saying, "Yes, Mom, you have told me three times that you are washing your towels," she heard me say, "Are you getting dementia like your mother?"

The point is, we have a hard enough time communicating important things with in-person nuances and emotions. Using our cool technology only makes that harder. It may seem easier and quicker, but how many times have you had to spend a lot longer than the few seconds it took to send a text to undo what the other person thought you meant?

Then we have those pesky emotions. They affect the way we hear something. Remember the last time you were stressed out and walked in the door after a very long day, and the first thing you heard was, "What's for dinner?" or "Did you remember to take out the garbage?"

The question is fine. It is not necessarily meant with any malice. Because of our emotional state, we can take it completely wrong and then reply with the wrong words or actions, or worse, silence, which is a very potent form of non-communication in situations like these. Our emotions and those of the other person can greatly affect our ability to communicate.

Lastly, literal noise or distractions keep us from communicating. There is a joke that if your partner is watching an intense sports event, it is a good time to ask them for anything you want. "Can I go to Mexico with my girlfriends?" or "Honey, can we talk about adopting a cat?"

Literal noise could have been at play in the loss of nearly 600 lives in an airplane accident where the pilot did not accurately hear what the air traffic controller was saying. I'm sure you have experienced trying to talk at a loud event, had to guess what the other person was saying, and likely nodded to something that might very well have been inappropriate.

We get that communication is hard. We get that. I'm really getting a clear idea that I need to improve my communication. So, what do we do about this? How can we alter the way we communicate to make us more effective? How can we remember the dozens of nuances of communication?

We often think that communication is all about the words we use and how we say those words. We may spend hours pondering how best to talk about a subject, but good communication is actually more about listening to ourselves, our own intent, and what we really want—and then listening to the other person, taking in their background, feelings, and how they're hearing what we are saying.

The Greek philosopher Epictetus said, "We have two ears and one mouth, so we should listen twice as much as we speak." It's a good rule.

The best way to improve our communication is by simply listening. Learn to listen to ourselves and to others, and we can all start to communicate better and hopefully produce less material for comedians about misunderstandings. It may not be as funny, but it would make life much easier.

Fifteen Seconds to Change Your World

That takes us to our fifteen-second action of the week. Today's fifteen-second action is contemplative. We're going to think about the person we would like most to improve our communication with. We're doing that so that for the rest of the book, we can think specifically about how to do that with them based on what we are learning today.

My Fifteen Seconds

I want to work on communication with my daughter because she's soon going to be a teenager. It could get harder to communicate with her. I don't want to lose the closeness with her.

So, I want to improve our communication now, and hopefully it will help us through her teenage years.

Citations and references for this chapter are located at the end of the book.

Four

It all started in 1904 in Berlin, Germany, where a mathematics teacher named Wilhelm von Austin taught a horse to count. It became known as the Clever Hans phenomenon, and you can even read about it today. For four years, Wilhelm trained Hans, the horse, to count people, tell time, identify specific playing cards, and he even appeared to know what a calendar was. The horse would tap his hooves to count or indicate the correct answer. It was remarkable and entertained lots of people. There were the obvious claims of fraud, but after an exhaustive scientific study in 1907, it was determined that there was no hoax or fraud.

However, that was not the end of the story. Hans, the horse, could not actually count. In 1907, it was discovered that Hans couldn't answer questions if the person asking the question did not know the answer, or if Hans could not see the person's face.

What was discovered was almost as amazing as the counting horse. You see, Hans could read minute subtle clues in the person asking the questions, and when the correct answer was presented, he would react to the facial expressions. Hans was so good at this that even if the person asking the questions tried to hide the answer, he could not—even the doctor who discovered this amazing fact.

It turns out that horses are so good at reading human faces that the smallest giveaway in facial expression tells the horse the answer. It is remarkable that animals can read us like that, but it also means that the horse couldn't really count.

Being able to count matters. You see, if you are a small fish in a big ocean, it is unlikely you will survive. If you're a small fish in a small group of fish... same answer. If you're a small fish in a *huge* school of fish, survival is more likely. Small fish are attracted to and then join large groups of their fellow fish.

Did you know that gray wolves will only hunt specific prey if there are enough of them? It takes six to eight wolves to hunt an elk successfully. For a bison, though, over nine are required. On the other side of the hunt, the elk tend to create smaller herds, attracting less attention, or much larger ones for protection.

Dogs, monkeys, and crows all can "count." I'm quoting the word "count" because it appears they can distinguish fairly easily between one and four of a thing. After four, however, things get very generalized. There are either lots more or fewer of something.

Scientists created a word for this: numerosity. The word refers to the ability to perceive numbers without directly counting. In other words, you recognize rather quickly that four dogs look different than five. Babies as young as a few months old act surprised when you magically make four apples turn into three or five into ten. It is called numerosity, or number sense, and it explains the mind's ability to notice a general idea of the number of an item.

An article by *Live Science* talks about humans' innate ability to calculate numbers without counting, and in some people, it can be so pronounced that it is like a sixth sense. They're called "number savants." However, you don't need to be a savant to look at a package of cookies and know an approximate or even exact number per row.

My daughter would argue that point. In my house, cookies regularly disappear, and I notice there are fewer and fewer, though she denies eating them. But that is another episode.

Whether it is determining the number of ships on the horizon or cookies in a jar, new research shows that the human brain has a map for *perceiving* numbers, which is a different area of the brain from that responsible for actual counting.

It is a sense, a specific part of the brain that does these cognitive calculations, and advertisers regularly use this sense to sell us things. When you see an ad that says its product has helped millions of people, that is numerosity. It is not a specific number, but we get the sense that they are talking about a lot of people, and that is supposed to convince us to buy the product.

Numerosity can help you to decide how to deal with a problem. If you are a football player running with the football, your brain can tell you without counting that there are more defensive players in one area than in another. In fact, it might even tell you an exact number.

"Six players are coming at me over there and five over here." That is helpful information in the split second it takes for your brain to tell you that, and you can do that without counting them on your fingers.

With animals, this information is also necessary but more limited. As mentioned, many animals can count up to four; after that, it is mostly just the sense that there is more food in one spot, or fewer predators in that area.

Animal brains are not designed to handle complex numbers or planning, which is exclusively the realm of humans. It's only one of the many ways that humans are substantially different from our fellow Earth inhabitants. I bring that up for a reason. Animals and humans are both greatly impacted by our interactions with each other and with the planet. However, humans have the capability to destroy our planet through selfish or unthinking actions. That also means we have a much greater responsibility.

Looking around, it seems we often forget we are indeed responsible for our world. That is perhaps because we feel less and less connected to the world around us, both intentionally—like building skyscrapers that isolate us in concrete jungles—and unintentionally, by the overuse of social media or technology. All those things have resulted in fewer connections. When we're less connected, we do not feel responsible for protecting or nurturing. It is like the saying that you never give a name to an animal raised for food. In this case, we *should* give names to the things around us, as we would care better for them.

Humans, by design, have advanced reasoning and problem-solving capabilities. We can imagine building a bridge over a channel of water, like the Golden Gate Bridge in San Francisco, then putting together the engineering, construction, and materials to make that happen. We can think about how planting a million trees will affect carbon dioxide concentrations in a hundred years, and carry that out even if the original planners have passed away.

In Oxford, England, there is a dining hall in New College. It was built with huge oak beams that they knew would last hundreds of years, but would eventually give out. The planners of the original building planted a grove of trees at the same time as the building, so that hundreds of years later, future generations would have the material to rebuild. That is amazing. Animals do not have that planning capability.

Humans have a complex language that comes with communication skills that go way beyond anything in the animal world. Animals do communicate. Whales and several other species have complex communication systems. However, humans alone have created grammar and syntax to communicate clearly. We go way beyond those basic skills when we discuss abstracts, the past, and possible future scenarios. For instance, merely *the idea* that humans are different from animals is an abstract thought. I can not only think that thought, but can also have an in-depth conversation about it.

We can talk about the past with emotions and lessons attached to it. For instance, to teach a lesson of modesty, a parent might relate the story of Uncle Bob, who attempted and failed to become a trapeze artist, as he had only one leg, was blind, and had diabetes. We could use the same story to teach the ability to overcome adversity. Then, we could hypothetically add that Uncle Bob actually thought he was a superhero and could fly, and we still don't know if he realized he wasn't and couldn't. That's pretty crazy when you think about it—not just about Bob becoming a trapeze artist, but our ability to turn him into multiple lessons and create a narrative that didn't even exist previously.

As humans, we do some pretty crazy things with our abstract thoughts. We use emojis to symbolize emotions. An animal would not understand if you showed an emoji of a carrot and a stick together, but humans can assign a meaning to it. We not only can do this, but we intentionally do so to make sure our nonverbal communication comes across in texts and emails. How many times are you ready to send a message, then reread and realize that the sentence might be taken in a different manner than intended? Maybe you added an emoji to make sure you didn't make your parents, spouse, or boss mad at you.

We can create symbols to represent something. Think of "XO" widely used to mean "hugs & kisses," but then can be interpreted based on context to mean "love you." Think of a red heart. What does that mean when it's used in a text? Here is an odd one. Make a V sign with your forefinger and middle finger. That symbol can mean "victory," "two," or "peace." Try to explain those differences to your dog, but contextually, we know what it means. When the ice cream server asks you how many scoops, if you give them that sign, do they think it means "peace?"

Right around 1968, you might have made that sign driving down the highway, to signal that you'd seen a yellow and pink VW bus. That is pretty cool and disturbing at the same time, that our minds understand symbols in the context they're given.

The concept of time is also unique to humans and one of the most difficult to understand. Animals somewhat understand days and seasons, but using a clock to measure time to tell us when to sleep and get up, when to eat, and when to go to work is all human thinking.

Our individual concept of time can be quite different. I'm sure you know people who say they have no concept of time. That may not be true, as they can very likely tell what time it is. However, in a practical way, they might live their lives as if time didn't matter. Humans can imagine themselves in a week, a month, or a year, especially when they are looking forward to something. Ask any girl how many times they have imagined what their wedding would be like, and you'll understand what I'm saying. Sometimes they have worked everything out to the color of the ribbons on the favors.

"I Think I Lost a Day"

This concept of time also works against us. Have you ever felt like you lost a day? Like the world forgot to tell you that today is actually yesterday, or tomorrow was today? Have you ever woken up in a hotel room and swore that you were in a different city?

Well, I have. So, I wrote a song about it. It is called "I Think I Lost a Day," and it's about this very feeling.

People who travel a lot say they experience this quite often, but honestly, I regularly get to Friday and swear I missed a couple of days somewhere. Sometimes I lose a couple of hours just by opening my phone. Technology is another place where we are very, very different than animals. Do you see anyone attempting to show bunnies how to avoid predators by playing video games on an iPad or even showing them pictures of what predators are? They're more likely to literally sit on it because it's warm.

Humans not only use technology, but they also create it, often without thinking of its consequences. Someone 125 years ago thought it would be a great idea to replace horses with a gasoline engine. That technology is really cool. But what have we done to ourselves? Over one million people and two billion animals die each year in car accidents.

Technology is unique to humans in several ways. We're the only species that creates it, but our creations often have very unintended consequences because we either choose not to or *cannot* see the future correctly.

You would think we could do that. As humans, we have the unique ability to think about ethical and moral guidelines. Whether or not those are popular, they are a part of who we are. We know it is wrong to hurt someone, to lie, and to steal. When we see people get away with such things, we get upset. That is why a two-year-old starts saying, "That's not fair!" We have a built-in sense of justice.

Strangely, as humans, we can feel guilty for stuff we haven't even done. Just imagining or thinking about doing something we know is wrong can cause us to feel bad or to confess. Many religions even require you to confess to wrong thoughts. Why would we even consider that? Because most humans actually want to be the best people we can be. We feel better when our conscience is clear. We are healthier, happier, and live longer without the burden of guilt.

We can think and plan about positive things as well. Humans create foundations and charities with the intent of helping people for years into the future. We can make a presentation on how doing or changing certain behaviors will make people happier, like helping people smile, which is my goal. My foundation, the World Smile Initiative *(www.worldsmileinitiative.org)*, was created with that intent. I can picture how my neighborhood could be transformed if everyone smiled more, and that makes me happy and encourages me to keep going.

We, as humans, are markedly different from animals. Although putting food in a dog's dish undoubtedly makes them happy, they cannot envision giving food to all the neighborhood dogs, nor do they want to. If you have two dogs, and you put food in both their bowls, but one eats both before the other dog, is there any guilt involved?

When a hummingbird chases off another hummingbird from eating from a flower, do either of them show concern or remorse for their actions? Humans not only have hardwired moral guidance, but they also enact laws and penalties for not following it. To show you how much we think about such things, just look up if yelling "fire" in a crowded theater is protected by free speech. The answers you'll find have a lot of ifs, ands, and buts. Why? It depends on so many things, including intent, harm, and cost. It takes into account if it was a mistake, how old you are, and a host of other things. You could argue this case in front of a jury, and depending on the nuances, you could be found guilty or not guilty.

Speaking of which, although most people use them interchangeably, there is a difference between "not guilty" and "innocent"—both a legal difference and a practical one. Again, a group of monkeys isn't going to sit around and argue that point for eight hours. On the other hand, humans do so regularly because we realize that without morals and ethics, we are no different than animals. We inherently feel that we have a higher standard to meet. We enact justice systems and punishments to make sure we maintain a higher standard of moral excellence.

Why do we do these things? Because we analyze our thoughts and emotions in the context of actions. We realize there is a difference between accidentally and intentionally hurting someone. This is also exactly why it is so hard to judge another human. We cannot read each other's thoughts or emotions. Rather, we have to guess based on external factors.

Animals do not sit around pondering their motivations or the motivations of Fred, who stole a banana from Martha. There is no deliberation about whether Fred was hungry, whether he took it to feed his child, or whether Martha owed him the banana. There is only the fact that Fred took a banana from Martha, and the consequences to Fred.

Beavers can build enormous dams and ten-foot-tall hills with long tunnels. Humans go way beyond that. Humans often manipulate their environment just to prove they can do it for no other purpose than pride or because they can.

Beavers don't compete with each other to have the biggest, highest, or deepest dams; there is no contest or award for sustainable construction. (Well, first of all, because they use only sustainable construction.) In reality, they're only building the dams because instinct told them to.

Humans, on the other hand, label their achievements as the biggest, tallest, or most sustainable. We are conscious of both our own thoughts and the thoughts of others. Some of us feel the need to give others a reason to remember us. At its most basic, though, we do those things to connect with other people, even if that only means other people knowing our name long after we are gone. Some people are so driven by that idea that they strategize generations ahead in planning to be remembered. Ants do not build an anthill to be remembered, nor do bees put their names on their honey hives, yet the human who cares for the honey will put their name on it.

Chimpanzees are nearly 99 percent genetically similar to humans. In that 1 percent, though, there is a massive gulf, not only in our incredible brains, but physically as well. For instance, our vocal cords are designed for complex speech. The difference between our vocal cords and animals' is like a wooden drum compared to a grand piano. They can both make similar sounds, but the difference is in the nuances. Someone may point out that parrots can speak. That is true, but they do not generate language with grammar, meaning, imagination, and self-reflection. They never wonder who they are out loud or in a 1,000-page book, but plenty of humans have.

Although we are 99 percent similar to chimpanzees and 97 percent to pigs, it's akin to saying that a ten-tier cake is 98 percent flour, sugar, and butter. I'd really be all into eating a ten-tier vanilla and chocolate cake with buttercream frosting... not so much a plate of flour, sugar, and butter. Even if they are 98 percent similar, the difference is in how they are put together.

As mentioned before, with the vast differences between animals and us, we have a much greater responsibility. Why? Because we can be more responsible. We can and should always choose to strive to be better and have a higher standard. If we all end up living like wild animals, only selfishly looking out for ourselves and maybe our immediate family, we will lose our humanity—not only who we are, but who we could become. We would lose our chance at happiness along with it.

If you ask anyone on earth what they want, 99.9999 percent of them will simply say they want to be happy. Well then, despite what the commercial world would tell us, neither money nor power, nor fame makes us truly happy. We know deep down what it takes to be happy.

We have to have our basic physical needs taken care of, and then we must feel connected to others and the nature around us. Most of all, we must feel love. We accomplish these things in remarkably simple actions like showing gratitude, smiling, reminding people that you love them, and being kind and playful. Doing those very small actions on a daily basis will transform our world. It may not alleviate the pressures of living in this world, but it will make them endurable because we have reason to look forward to each day, and we have a higher purpose.

In the grand adventure of life, humans stand alone, not because we are the strongest or the fastest, but because we are the only species that contemplates our own existence and shapes the world in profound ways. The question is not just what makes us different, but what we choose to do with that difference.

Will we use our unique abilities to uplift and innovate, or will we squander them on selfish pursuits? The answer lies in each one of us, because to be human is not just to think, it is to dream, to create, and to bring the world a better moment than the one before it.

~~~~~~~~~~~~~~~

I remember being in school and my teacher loudly interrupting my constant daydreaming. I much preferred being in my daydream. It was a happier place. So, in the next chapter, I'm going to take us back into a place where my daydreams lived. I hope you will join me there.

Fifteen Seconds to Change Your World

We've done gratitude actions before, but today we want to be grateful for something about our amazing body. Maybe you appreciate that you can pick a flower, hold your child, or use your imagination to make a poem. It could be because you are in love or feel loved by someone. Maybe because you are excited about your future, or you remember a particular moment in your past that makes you happy.

Perhaps it is because you love music as I do, or cooking, or walking
~~~~~~~~~~~~~~~

your dog. Whatever it is, take a moment to be grateful for our bodies. It makes us happier, reduces stress, and makes life richer and more purposeful.

My Fifteen Seconds

I'm grateful for my amazing body because it regrew my liver after I lost 60 percent of it in a lifesaving liver resection surgery. I can enjoy a quality life, and it means I can be here and share my thoughts with you today.

Citations and references for this chapter are located at the end of the book.

Daydreaming: A Superpower

I must have been only two or three years old when my parents would leave me at home by myself. When they returned hours later, I would be in the same place they left me. I didn't need to wander out of the apartment to go on an adventure. I simply disappeared into my mind to visit a world where I had pets, was playing outside, and eating fun food I wanted.

I always thought my daydreaming was bad, so I never told anyone about it. I got really good at it to the point that I could mentally disappear during almost any stressful situation, whether at home, school, work, or while having relationship issues. It became as much a protection for me as it was recreation.

Nowadays, my daydreaming is more about reviewing the day's events or conversations. For instance, we once had company over for dinner and enjoyed a wonderful conversation about topics I talk about on the Make Me Smile podcast. However, I forgot to ask them questions that I really would have liked to hear their answers to, so my brain took me back to the conversation where I could ask those questions and get my answers. When I do that, even though I'm only daydreaming, I feel satisfied, and my brain can let the conversation go.

I also do that often when watching TV shows. If I find myself involved in a conversation on screen but the characters in the show don't answer some questions or have conversations that I really would like them to have, I will ask those questions in my mind to get the answers I want.

I find it enlightening and fun, but now that I'm saying it out loud, I'm worried I'm the only one who does this. In fact, in the middle of that thought, I just disappeared to a pretend recording session with Tony and Mimy Succar for a new Latin song I wrote called "Feel the Heat." Mimi and I were laughing and having lots of fun recording.

A few minutes before I started recording this episode, I heard that a famous person was going to attend the Oscars. I found myself transported to what I imagined that event would be like, and in my daydream, I noticed someone with an amazing hairstyle. That took me to a hair salon, having my own hair done, and shopping for the dress I had just seen.

I can accomplish an awful lot in a matter of moments in my daydreams. Some people may say I'm using my imagination rather than daydreaming. However, daydreaming has less direction and takes on a life of its own. Imagination is more directed. In other words, if I want to picture a unicorn with a pink saddle jumping over the moon, I can do that using my imagination. Now that I put that picture in your head, you may find that the unicorn takes off on its own and enters its own storyline, having conversations without you actively directing it. Well, that is daydreaming.

I used to think that only children daydreamed, but I realized I've been doing it my whole life. I can lose a few minutes or even hours thinking about everything from a food I wish I were eating to an animal I would like to play with. Sometimes, I spend the time with a happy or even embarrassing moment from my past.

I really didn't understand why I seemed to have such a tendency to do this, so I thought I would do some reading and listening, and I was so surprised that what I call inspiration or creating music is really a form of daydreaming. When I feel an emotion, my mind plays a miniature movie that takes on a life of its own. That movie is accompanied by an original song that just pops into my head most of the time, almost complete. I just didn't realize that it was daydreaming, but it is. Part of my reluctance to admit that I daydream stems from my childhood. I was told to stop daydreaming all the time. If I was supposed to be focused on the lesson at hand, the game I was supposed to be playing, or the work I was supposed to do, I could disappear into my head until an adult or another schoolmate rudely pulled me out of it. Even today, there is a common term in China—rumination. It has a negative connotation, relating to overthinking a positive future or a past situation. We'll talk about that kind of daydreaming later. It can be unhealthy if overdone.

However, the general feeling about it in China is negative, and that implication covers daydreaming, in both good forms and bad. That results in reluctance to talk about daydreaming in a positive way.

Throughout most of my life, I found that I much preferred the world in my head to the world outside it—reality—so when someone forced me back to real life, I was reluctant. Honestly, I might then do the task I was supposed to do, but my mind would drift right back to where I was before in my head. Sometimes that was floating on a cloud, picking flowers, bothering a bug, or sitting on my dad's lap, singing songs.

What I didn't know is that my brain could kind of do both things because of the Default Mode Network (DMN). I've talked about this network before, during the chapter on awe. The DMN in our brain activates when we're not engaged in a specific task. Think of it as a brain autopilot. It monitors critical things while our brain visits other worlds, solves problems, plans, and reflects.

If you have ever been driving and realized you didn't remember the last 10 miles, well, thank the DMN for keeping you relatively safe. I'm not intentionally daydreaming while driving, but if I do, my DMN can still operate the car even when my brain is somewhere else.

Interestingly, the DMN is not active during deep sleep. What we dream during rapid eye movement (REM) is not daydreaming, but something else altogether. Daydreaming happens, as the name indicates, during times when we're awake. Sometimes our brain does this without a conscious effort, but we can also do it intentionally.

For instance, assuming you're in a safe place right now, think about what it would feel like lying on a float in a pool with a drink in your hand, music playing in the background, with the sun setting behind you. Then let your mind drift to what you would do next, or who you are with, or a feeling. That is daydreaming. Now, please come back to me and don't stay in your daydream. Still, it shows you that we can intentionally daydream.

Why do we do it? Evidently, it is a way for us not only to imagine impossible things, but it also helps us process experiences, anticipate actions, make connections, and plan.

For instance, we can feel embarrassed after an event happens. Picture going to the bathroom and finding out later that day you had toilet paper hanging out of your pants. Makes me cringe just mentioning it! In reality, there is nothing to be embarrassed about at that moment because that event happened hours ago, but we can feel our cheeks flush, and we might want to crawl under our bed for a bit. On the good side, it may make you keep a mental note to check your pants after using the bathroom from then on.

Perhaps you have a meeting with your boss tomorrow. You can daydream or imagine what that meeting might be like. You can rehearse in your head what you say, how to say it, and how you'll react. You might even mentally try on different outfits to see how that changes the anticipated meeting. That is a great use of daydreaming.

We can daydream about who we would like to have over to our place or imagine taking a walk with someone and seeing what happens. People who have spent a lot of time isolated may create imaginary friends or associates to spend time with. If you have watched the movie A Beautiful Mind, you've seen how imaginary friends can help us through difficult situations. The mind uses its ability to daydream to offer protection from situations that might make us literally crazy. I have talked about this concept before and mentioned the movie

Cast Away. Tom Hanks uses daydreaming to create a friend out of a volleyball, which he names Wilson. Wilson, an imaginary friend, helps him to avoid going crazy.

Children who are abused often will disassociate. I did this as a child when I would get beaten. Children's minds can create a better world for themselves than the one they're experiencing until they must return to their unfortunate situation. In all these cases, daydreaming can be a powerful way to protect ourselves.

I especially use daydreaming when writing music. I can be watching something that triggers an emotion, and suddenly I'm transported to not just that scene, but the entire emotional situation that plays out in my head. I can see, hear, touch, and feel the emotions of the scene. It is because of those daydreams that songs come out of me.

This is my song, "If Love Was Just a Game."

"If Love Was Just a Game"

This song takes place in an imaginary world that I got caught up in one day. It's about falling in love with someone that I know I will never be with, but in my mind, I was playing a character in a game, and I wanted to win the king, my future husband. This song has not yet been released, but it has a really fun music video, and with this QR code, you can watch it.

Daydreaming allows our subconscious mind to process experiences, make connections, and rehearse future situations. Children have this amazing gift to not only protect themselves but also cope with difficult situations. It's a way to explore possibilities, practice social scenarios in their head, and learn that there are worlds beyond what they can see with their eyes, but are attainable through their imagination. That daydreaming superpower can help a child become someone other than who they appear destined to become based on where or how they grew up.

A child who has never experienced anything but poverty, sickness, and war can imagine a world where they are free, healthy, and can create and inspire others. It is not limited to children. Adults have this ability too. Even if we are in a situation we have never experienced, we can use daydreaming to discover ways to overcome it or learn to tolerate it. People with life-threatening ailments like cancer can and have used the power of daydreaming to help them endure, heal, and even overcome. Science has repeatedly shown that positive thinking has a measurable effect on our health.

Daydreaming about positive things alleviates stress, lowers anxiety, reduces pain, and boosts our immune system response. It also simply makes us feel better in everyday life. Creative people regularly use daydreaming. They may not call it that, but they use it to create. Salvador Dalí, the famous surrealist artist, was perhaps the most direct in using daydreaming to unlock his subconscious and to create surreal worlds of time and space, as shown in his art forms. Albert Einstein is reported to have daydreamed about riding and running beside a sunbeam to the edge of the universe, which gave him the idea of the theory of relativity.

Some of the most famous fiction authors used daydreaming to conjure up characters, scenes, and an entire new world for us to explore with them. Ninety-two percent of fiction writers say that their characters act on their own, and they are sometimes surprised at what they do.

My husband, who has written multiple novels, says that his characters take on a life of their own, and he is often surprised by what they say or how they act in the story. Of course, that really can't be true because the characters come from the imagination of the author. However, daydreaming allows those characters to have their own lives seemingly independent from the author.

I would say that is almost crazy sounding, but of course, I experience that when I create music. I do not know where it comes from. It just is there, almost as if it has its own will. In fact, if I do not write music regularly, it feels as if my emotions get stuck or are blocked. My emotions need to have an outlet, which explains why, for the first thirty-four years of my life—the time when I didn't know I could write music—I was emotionally impaired or suppressed.

Writing releases our minds to daydream and lets out our emotions in healthy, fun, and productive ways. There is that thing called writer's block, but it doesn't just happen to writers. Have you ever been working at something for a long time and just can't seem to grasp it? Whether it was writing a report, preparing for a meeting, having a conversation, or even planning a big event. Then you step away from it for a while, and the solution or answer just drifts into your mind. That is an example of how our minds take advantage of daydreaming to create solutions and solve problems. It does that without us asking or directing it. In fact, trying to direct or ask for it often hinders the solution from coming to us. Daydreaming is amazing.

Daydreaming can also help us prepare. There was a famous Canadian pianist, Glen Gould, who was known for his mental, not physical, preparation for recording. He didn't need to play the actual piano, but would play the composition in his head. In fact, he would intentionally mentally rehearse pieces without physically playing them until shortly before the recording session.

Amazingly, MRI scans have shown that mentally practicing and physically practicing light up the same areas of the brain. It is common practice with sports athletes, including those participating in Olympic events and professional sports. They use visualizations or imagery as training tools. They can practice running races, including unexpected events, throwing, hitting, and shooting, all in their heads. This type of training has been consistently shown to be productive during the actual event.

Mentally practicing in car racing is critical. Performance coach Ross Bentley says, "The best drivers can visualize every inch of a circuit. If you can't, then you're leaving something on the table, and you'll get beaten by others who have developed this skill. When I think of the best drivers that I've coached—drivers of all levels, but the ones who win the most at whatever level and form of racing they're involved in—they are all better at visualization than the drivers they beat most often." On a more basic level, daydreaming can help prepare us to make friends. When we were children, we often had imaginary friends. We would talk, spend time with them, and go on adventures. As we get older, making friends can sometimes be difficult, but by imagining how we could start a friendship, what it would be like, and how we might enjoy it, we can open up those possibilities.

All of these types of visualization are forms of daydreaming. Dr. James Comer says, "Daydreaming is not a waste of time, but rather a needed escape to help us function better." I wholeheartedly agree. Daydreaming is not just optional; it is required for our brains to function optimally. Our brains are not designed for constant focus. It would be like driving your car like a race car driver every minute of every day. Expect something to break down if you do that. Same with our brain. It needs downtime. When we overwork our brains, they actually might shut down on us without letting us know.

Have you ever been in an intense study or work session, and you realize you lost five or ten minutes? That is your brain telling you that you are overheating and need a break, so it just shuts you down during those moments. It is the DMN that takes over. To everyone else, it might look like you are still hard at it, but in reality, your brain just took you on a mandatory trip to Tahiti. It's kind of like getting told to sit in the corner until you are treating your brain nicer.

We've talked about how daydreaming can help with creativity and problem-solving, but it also helps with our emotions. For instance, in the case of feeling embarrassed hours after something happened, we can imagine that no one noticed or that it didn't really happen. Basically, rewriting history to our benefit. Our brains can make us feel better by pretending.

It can also help us with other emotions such as compassion, confidence, and even love. Let's say we fought with a friend or a family member. After we have cooled down, we may decide that we overreacted—or maybe not—but it allows us to reimagine how things might have been handled differently and gives us a chance to reflect on what is really important. We can explore how the feelings we had at that heated moment may not have been accurate or how valuable the relationship with the other person is to us, helping us heal or motivating us to repair the relationship.

We can also use daydreaming to imagine how it feels to achieve a goal. Perhaps we imagine graduating, completing a small or basic task, or getting the 'thank you' or appreciation that we deserve. That imagined thought can create motivation to keep going, and when we feel depressed, imagining how we can be of help to others if we endure and find a way through can help us see a different future.

We can lift our own spirits simply by imagining smiling at someone, getting a smile in return, acting silly, or seeing people be happy. Those are all things daydreaming can do to help us recharge and unwind, as well as repair and heal.

~~~~~~~~~~~~~~~~

We've talked a lot about the positive aspects of daydreaming, but just like with any gift, we can also abuse this superpower. If we daydream at inappropriate times or about unhealthy things, it can be hurtful to us. For example, social media promotes materialistic daydreaming by showing us people living supposedly glamorous lives. If we spend time daydreaming about being rich or famous, we could literally miss out on living our lives and enjoying the wonderful things around us, and instead become discontent and unhappy. That
~~~~~~~~~~~~~~~~

would not be a good use of daydreaming. We could also find ourselves ruminating. That is the idea of getting caught in a mental loop. This can be seeing ourselves in bad, embarrassing, or unhealthy situations and reliving them over and over again. Unlike the movie Groundhog Day, this kind of repeated mental experience can leave us feeling fatigued and defeated. It is neither funny nor healthy.

~~~~~~~~~~~~~~~

I interviewed someone named Stefan for this chapter and asked him whether he daydreamed as a child. Stefan told me that not only did he daydream as a child, but he intentionally does so as an adult.

Stefan noted that it helps his mindset throughout the day in order to remain optimistic and willing to embrace good things. On the flip side, Stefan admitted that daydreaming creeps in at times when it shouldn't, like when speaking to a customer.

~~~~~~~~~~~~~~~

So, while daydreaming is a superpower, just like any power, it must be used correctly to help and heal instead of hurt and break down. Used properly and regularly, daydreaming can not only be fun and productive, but it can also fuel us to become better people, live more fulfilling lives, and help those around us reach higher heights.

The next time you find yourself daydreaming, embrace the journey. Perhaps you will find your best idea, your brightest creation, or your most satisfying moment, beginning with the amazing world inside your mind.

Fifteen Seconds to Change Your World

Today, our fifteen-second call to action is easy and fun. Practice daydreaming for a moment, if it is safe for you. To do so, I'm going to start you out with a story, and you take it from there.

It's a perfect summer day. You're sitting with your favorite person, watching a sunset. The warm breeze gently touches your face, and you are mesmerized by the most beautiful scene unfolding in front of you.

What did you see?

My Fifteen Seconds

I saw my family and me sitting on a grassy area by the ocean. There were lots of other people there, too—couples, families, kids, and dogs.

Our dog was lying on the grass facing the wrong way, looking confused and frustrated because everyone was looking at the sky instead of playing with her. She was put out.

Citations and references for this chapter are located at the end of the book.

Episode 18

Hope: A Promise to Our Future

No matter what you think about rats, this true story is remarkable. In the 1950s, a researcher named Kurt Richter put a group of wild, fierce rats into a jar of water. The rats had no way to escape, and within a few minutes, they all gave up and started drowning, at which point the researcher rescued them. He then waited a while, gave them a bit of comfort, and put the same rats back in the water. This time, there was a remarkable change. The rats kept swimming for days. What was the difference? Hope. The knowledge that someone might rescue them kept them going and going and going.

Hope is an incredible, powerful emotion. It can defy reason and logic and propel us to do things we didn't think were possible. All we need is the smallest glimpse of possibility, whether real or imagined, and that glimmer can keep us sustained for days, years, or even decades.

There has been much written about hope and tons of speculation as to why we have it. We do know that it is hardwired in many creatures, but especially in humans. It is a gift to us. It is the reason we overcome adversity, and it gives us the strength to keep working toward a goal.

Without hope, we would give up in the face of difficulty. I noticed this one day when a hummingbird had hurt itself and was on the ground. As I reached toward it, it tried to hobble away, but immediately gave up when I picked it up.

It was as if it was saying, "OK, my life is over. I guess this is it." It was so sad. As I talked to it and stroked it gently, it started to react positively, gaining energy until it got up and flew off. It was a wonderful moment of awe, like I've talked about previously, but it also showed how creatures, including us, would react if they didn't have hope. We would give up, resign ourselves to whatever was happening, and eventually that would result in our death. Of course, that is not the case. We have this inherent gift from birth. When a child is in need, they cry for attention, hoping someone will help. When a toddler is in need, he or she will immediately call for his or her mom or dad, having hope that they will come to their rescue.

As we get older, we tend to internalize our hope more, but it is there, and it is very strong. Remember taking a test that you were not prepared for and hoping that, by some miracle, you did better than was realistic?

How about when you applied for your first loan, and you sat there hoping it would get approved, even though you likely had no credit? What about your first relationship? Did you have eyes full of hope as to what your future was together?

Even as we go into our sunset years, we continue to hope. We hope our children will be happy. We hope our annual checkups are all clear, even though we might have stopped exercising and have eaten unhealthy food for the last year or two or three.

Our lives are literally full of things we hope for, and things we hope don't happen to us. When things have very special potential, either good or bad, we hope even harder. It is said there are no atheists in the foxholes. What that really means is that even when things look horribly bad, we will hold out for miraculous hope.

Likewise, if you are reading a book or watching a movie, and starting to enjoy the story, as you get more and more involved, you find yourself hoping for certain outcomes. How many times have you been devastated that something didn't happen the way you hoped?

Hope often intensifies when things are really good or really bad. It is especially potent to us if our lives have another special component. If we have something to look forward to, a purpose in our life, then hope takes on multiple aspects that involve more than us.

For instance, a person who has a small child or someone who loves them has an additional reason to keep pushing. If they find themselves capsized in a lake, they will immediately start hoping for help, or that they can swim to shore, or that someone will see them. Add on a specific purpose in life, like a child dependent on them, or perhaps they are deeply in love with someone, then it gives them even more reason to fight to live. They may even consciously say, "I need to survive for my son" or "I'm going to survive because I love my fiancé and I have to see them." Or perhaps a medical researcher may say, "I'm so close to curing cancer, I must survive."

We don't call it hope at that moment, but that is what it is. This teaches us something very important. Human connection and a sense of purpose are critical components to making it through difficult times, and to give us strength when needed. However, in the water, struggling to survive is not the time to look for our purpose or find that person. Those connections, those loved ones, have to be a part of our lives before those situations happen. Making those human bonds and feeling that we are living with purpose are things we must do now. They give us reason to keep going even under the most difficult of situations.

Finding time to build strong relationships is not easy. We all go through periods of time where we do better at this than others. In this crazy world with so many pressures and distractions, it seems we have forgotten that spending time with our loved ones to connect is more important than being on our electronic devices. I think we would all admit that we don't spend enough time talking with or planning to be with those we love or might want to love. Even right now, as I'm writing this, my family members are all in different rooms doing different things, and this is reminding me that I need to spend time with them.

When we don't have love in our lives, we feel aimless, and we often find ourselves doing things to fill that void we feel. Oftentimes, we focus on the wrong things. That need for connection and purpose gnaws at us like a mild hunger, but sometimes we don't recognize what it is. That listlessness, that slight sadness when we don't really have a reason to feel sad, that emptiness, that is us losing our hope!

Our brain and body are telling us we need to find a reason to believe in something or someone again. I was thinking about this feeling recently, and I wrote a song about it: "Give Me a Reason." I'd love to share it with you now because it is about this subject of hope.

There is a line there. "I won't hang on if you won't give me a reason to believe in you." I wrote that imagining a person who hoped to find love but didn't know how to find that person and wanted a reason to hang on. They needed hope that someone out there would believe in them and love them.

There are lots of songs about the search for love. Love gives us the strongest purpose and makes us feel the most hopeful, like anything is possible. That is why people who are in love liken it to walking on clouds, flying, or a feeling of invincibility. Love provides the strongest hope we can possibly experience.

Remember when I was talking about being stranded in a body of water and asked what thoughts would come to your mind? You likely would have thoughts about the people you love and your purpose in life. Those are powerful reasons to keep going. Just an interesting thought to see how our priorities get messed up—if you are actually drowning, do you believe in that moment you would think, "I need to survive for my social media followers" or "I need to live because I love my favorite video game so much"? Obviously not. You would be thinking of your life, the people you love, and your purpose. Yet what happens daily? When we are faced with the choice of spending time with our loved ones or time on our devices, what do we often choose? We all know the sad answer to that. Let's just say it leaves room for improvement, doesn't it?

Hope is more than just a strong emotion. It also helps us build and achieve things. We start companies and set goals because of the hope of success. That hope drives and propels us forward.

I have a friend who is starting a company building tiny homes. What he pictures is a time when no one is homeless. That hope, that vision, keeps pushing him forward, even though that goal is years away. A person who is going to make a six-course dinner may work on it all day or even for days because they hope the dinner is spectacular and that the guests love it.

The single pursuit of that dinner is often so simple—the hope that other people enjoy it. But if we didn't have that hope, would we make amazing meals? Would there be Michelin-rated restaurants? No, because without the hope of people enjoying the meal, no one would bother trying to make something spectacular. Without people to enjoy it, hardly anyone would cook fancy meals.

Those are the two components that hope uses as fuel: connections and the vision of something great. A sports team is started or bought for potentially billions of dollars, all based on hope. It is the hope that with the right people, the right talent, and the right timing, you can have a great team that wins games. If that hope didn't exist, people would no longer have sports teams, nor would many people attend games. It is hope that makes sports exist, and during a game, hope plays a huge part.

I love to play doubles badminton, and there are times when you find yourself behind, then all of a sudden you have a couple of good points and feel something happening inside. You smile more at your partner. Your concentration is stronger. You're a little more focused. You hustle a little bit more. Hope propels you forward. Games would be no fun if everyone just gave up all the time.

Have you ever seen a dog digging a hole in the backyard to escape? As they get deeper and deeper into the hole till their butt is the last thing you can see, what is happening? Their tail is wagging like crazy. Dirt is flying so fast, it looks as if someone turned on a dirt faucet. You know why. The dog can sense they're close. They're really close, and they get really excited. Now, what is the likelihood that the dog's going to give up at that point? No chance. It is the same thing with humans. Hope pushes us to finish. When we see the literal finish line, whether that is finishing washing the dishes or building a skyscraper, we get the expectation of feeling a sense of accomplishment, and we are driven even more to finish. That is hope.

I have some friends who have been married for decades but recently went through some serious difficulties in their relationship. We have all been there. In a situation like that, where you've had some pretty bad ups and downs, then one day something clicks and everything seems to be going well. You are talking more, holding hands, and smiling more. It feels like you have turned the corner. Is that the time you give up? No. Hope begets hope. It makes you want something more. You can taste and imagine what your life could be like when things are going right. That is hope.

Hope exists even if we know it doesn't really affect something. My dog sleeps outside my bedroom door. She is getting quite old, and I find that every morning before I open the door, I hope to see her get up and greet me.

I know that hoping won't change what actually happens, but that does not stop me from hoping every single day. You see, hope doesn't have to have logic behind it. It can be something we just imagine.

Amazingly, even if it is an imagined hope, it affects the way we live. Science has shown that positive thinking—hope—can help us when we're very sick, even with cancer. In fact, according to ScienceDirect, increased hope appears to predict a greater possibility of survival in advanced cancer. So, hope has a very real effect on us. This makes logical sense, too. If we give up hope, we stop trying. We stop smiling, we stop living, and we stop taking care of ourselves. It's like the first rats in the jars full of water. We give up, and that lets the disease, whether mental, emotional, or physical, win.

I have several friends who suffer from depression. It is a debilitating disease, and obviously, there can be chemical imbalances that cause it, but many times it is also due to circumstances in life. The one thing in common that they all say helps is when they try to focus on the idea that if they endure, they can be of help to others. The thought or hope that they could help someone else who suffers from depression is one of the strongest reasons they have to keep fighting. It is the hope that they can be of use to others that keeps them going.

There was another study from Harvard that focused on optimism and pessimism in coronary heart disease. Optimism is akin to hope, and pessimism is akin to having no hope. It involved a group of over 1,300 men who were chosen because they had an optimistic or pessimistic way of living. After ten years, it was found that around 160 of those men ended up with heart disease. Of those 160, how many do you think were the optimists versus the pessimists? It was two to one. Pessimists had twice as many occurrences of heart disease. Having hope, whether that meant they took better care of themselves or had less stress for whatever reason, cut the chance of heart disease in half.

Having hope is a healthier way to live. The book, *The Body Keeps the Score,* talks about an account that happened in 1924 with the famous researcher Ivan Pavlov. Pavlov made an accidental discovery relating to trauma and hope that year when the Neva River, in St. Petersburg, Russia, thawed. It caused a flood in Pavlov's basement laboratory, where there were a bunch of dogs in cages. The dogs were trapped in their cages as the cold water rushed in.

Before you panic, I want to say they all survived, but they paid a heavy price. The dogs' personalities changed dramatically. They were terrified even after the water receded, and they were released. A significant number of them, although not physically harmed, were emotionally broken. They acted depressed and would no longer interact with people.

Each dog had a different response. Some became very aggressive, and some despondent. Some, paradoxically, reacted positively when confronted with negative stimuli like the sound of rushing water— kind of like traumatized war veterans who go back to war because it is where they feel the most alive. Nearly every one of them was affected by their experience of hopelessness. That feeling of no way out altered their personalities for the rest of their lives.

That is a lesson for us as well. When we experience something so unjust and wrong that we feel utterly helpless, it can create anger and depression. It can also create an inability to form lasting relationships because our basic purpose to be loved and cared for has been violated. It can even create a tendency to seek out hopeless situations because that is what has been imprinted on us as normal.

Living a life like that can lead to depression, abuse, and a loss of will. Hope is so important to live and find a purpose in life, because it provides the vision of the life we truly feel entitled to. Hopelessness, thus, feels inherently wrong.

Unlike Pavlov's dogs, however, we can comprehend this emotional state. So what if we suffer from such trauma? How can we overcome that and give ourselves the right to have hope? It is amazingly basic. We build hope by doing things that are good for us. We can start with small things: eating well, getting regular exercise, setting small goals, practicing gratitude, and connecting with good people. I know it seems simplistic, but think about it for a second. We are designed to be connected to the earth and each other. When we're connected in mind, heart, and physically, we are meeting our purpose, and finding our purpose makes us feel good. So even though these are small actions, they are extremely powerful.

Don't forget about the connection between hopelessness and pessimism. Remember the study on those 1,300 men? Men who were pessimists suffered twice as often from heart disease as the optimists. Negative thinking is like rust. In the beginning, you hardly notice it, and sometimes, you might even think it's cool. Eventually, however, it corrodes and renders whatever it is eating away useless.

It is the same with pessimism. So let's not be fooled into thinking that being cynical or having a critical, pessimistic attitude is to be revered as an indication of intelligence. Actually, negative thinking demands little intellect. Have you ever noticed that when someone in a group starts complaining, everyone else does too? When someone starts speaking badly about a person, others often join in. It is so easy to slip into negative thinking and resign ourselves to the fact that we as a human race are hopeless.

I understand why people feel this way. There is much to feel sad and discouraged about, but despite how we might feel at this very moment, taking the time to read this today shows that there are people who really do care. So, let's choose to be hopeful. That is not being ignorant. It is being forward-looking, productive, and healthy.

Wouldn't it be amazing if we could help someone have more hope? You can't just go up and tell someone, "You should be hopeful." It doesn't work that way. Hope comes to us internally when we feel potential, connection, and have positive thoughts.

For us to create hope in ourselves or in others is like the movie

Inception. The idea has to come from deep inside yourself organically. You need to plant a seed that will grow the right kind of thought. A positive, happy, and uplifting idea.

Recently, I was meeting with some Gen Zers and talking about the need to feel gratitude. Their beautiful answers gave me hope for our future. When I see a young child reading a book or playing outside instead of looking at an electronic device, that gives me hope. We can actively look for hope in our own daily lives, like in the budding of the cherry blossoms. As I'm writing this, it's during this time of the year that, in many countries, the first wild flowers are starting to appear, giving us hope. Take a moment to enjoy that feeling, as it is contagious. Share a kind word with a stranger or a friend, and that will give you both hope.

Remember that hope has so many benefits. Hope changes our perspective and helps us overcome hardships. It helps us complete tasks even when things seem bleak. It's good for our mental and physical health, as shown by many studies. People who are hopeful experience less stress, anxiety, and depression. Hope boosts the immune system, too. Hope is not passive; it doesn't just think good thoughts, but it actively does them, like our fifteen-second action today.

Hope purposely tries to make our world a better place. When we feel hopeful, it strengthens our bonds with others, and when we feel hopeful, we work harder to have healthy relationships with those we care about. We seek connection and are encouraged to be around. Lastly, it gives us purpose and makes us more loving and lovable, which then creates more connections of hope in those we love.

In turn, those who feel love and hope spread it even further. It's a web of kindness, if you will, that can and will change your world. And it only takes a few seconds of our day.

Fifteen Seconds to Change Your World

What kind of actions bring hope? Simply being kind or saying a kind word can do this. You see, when we do these simple things, it makes the other person feel good, which allows them to think positively. They feel connected because someone noticed them, and that, in turn, can create hope—hope that they are not alone, that they are worthwhile, and that they have a place and purpose in the world.

If you are the one who needs hope, say a kind word to yourself right now. Try to do this in the mirror or with the phone turned on as a selfie. I know it feels awkward, but please just try it. "You did a great job at your work today. I appreciate that you always try to smile at people." Say something kind to yourself. If there is a worker who is trying hard, tell them that. If there is someone who looks amazing today, tell them you love their outfit. We just did this to three strangers in a mall, and they were smiling for the next five minutes.

Being kind always works because even if the person doesn't respond, you know you are doing something good. So, in the next fifteen seconds, say a kind word to yourself or someone else. If you can't do it at the moment, then determine to send a text, email, or better yet, a phone call to someone who could use it.

My Fifteen Seconds

I went to tell my husband, since he's the only one awake at nap time, "Thank you for doing all the preparation for our daughter's pool party tomorrow so I could be recording this episode of the podcast right now." He does a lot for our family and me every day. I never want to view it as something he should do. Rather, I want to show my appreciation for every big and little thing he does for us. I understand it doesn't take away any workload from him, but I believe it helps him to do these things with more joy, and it brings joy to my heart, too. It benefits both sides.

Citations and references for this chapter are located at the end of the book.

Play With Me

Have you ever watched a full-grown, reasonably intelligent adult play "peekaboo" with an infant? You know, when the adult gets in front of the infant's face, covers their own face with their hands, then suddenly removes them and says, "Peekaboo!" to a delighted baby. Adults do that over and over again, even to the point that others watching find it almost embarrassing. However, to the infant and adult involved, it feels absolutely perfect.

I got to wondering if that interaction, which is almost universal, is more than it appears. I was surprised—but not too surprised—to learn that there is a lot more going on here than literally meets the eye. Obviously, a connection forms between the infant and the adult, a huge benefit in itself. Playing together makes them both happy, so much so that the adult doesn't care what they look like.

The actions themselves are very important for the growth and mental capability of that baby. The baby is learning object permanence, a concept that is not inherent. The baby must learn that things and even people continue to exist even when they're out of view. This concept is crucial. A baby who doesn't understand this will experience extreme stress and anxiety when an adult in their lives walks out of a room. Perhaps you've had a pet that went through what we call "separation anxiety." The pet doesn't understand that when you walk through that front door, you're coming back, leading to serious misbehavior and even destruction.

One of the ways you can teach a pet that you are indeed still alive and coming back is to play a form of "peekaboo" with them. Leave through the door, then suddenly open it and reappear. Vary the time you wait before opening it, and the pet learns that just leaving the room doesn't mean you're leaving them forever.

Object permanence is a lifelong important concept; it provides stability to a child's world and helps them assign value to the things and people around them. There is no point in building a connection with things and people who are going to just leave.

Many studies have shown that humans, especially babies and young children, have lifelong issues if they lack connection. Playing "peekaboo" is one of the best ways to teach this concept of object permanence, but play in general goes way beyond that.

Children love to learn. It is often said that children are little imitators, but they're actually imitation experts. They do it actively. Your child or baby watches and studies you constantly to see how you do things. When they are able, they will immediately start imitating you. They will stand the way you do and wear the same clothes. They will even copy your facial expressions, checking to see if they are doing it like you are, then adjust if you adjust. They see this as play. Even though the adult might see it as work, to the baby, it is fun.

Dr. Stuart Brown from the National Institute for Play—and yes, that is a real institution—says, "The opposite of play is not work—the opposite of play is depression." Think about that for a second. If you ask most adults what the opposite of play is, they would say, "Work." Remember that for the child imitating you—whether it's cooking a meal, washing dishes, working on a car, or building a house—that is play to them. So work is not the opposite of play.

Think of this scenario: two people draw on a piece of paper. Both draw houses. One of them is working, and the other is playing. How do you tell?

Two people are riding a bicycle. One is working (or training), and the other is playing. How do you know the difference?

It is the attitude, isn't it? In fact, in Mark Twain's famous story of Tom Sawyer and Huckleberry Finn, Tom is tasked with painting a fence, but he convinces the other boys that he is having fun. Because of his fun attitude, they end up doing his work for him. Now, did finding out Tom's trick change the fact that the boys had fun?

You can also tell by facial expressions and body language how a person views the action they're doing. The person painting the fence for work, or training on a bicycle, will have very different non-verbal communication than a person playing. Watch children riding bicycles versus the Tour de France. Who is smiling, joking, and having fun... and who is working hard?

Play has mostly to do with our attitude, not our actions. If you ask a young child if they want to play, and they dejectedly say "no," you assume that the child is sad or depressed. Any happy child *always* wants to play.

Think of how that changes as an adult. If you ask an adult to play with you and they say no, you assume they're too busy or too important, but could it be they're really just not happy inside? Makes you wonder, doesn't it?

When you're playing and having fun, there can be a total loss of time and a vacating of responsibility. In other words, when we play, even adults have lots of fun. Time flies. The things that were so important before the play started just don't feel so important.

That is not a bad thing. In many cases, the brain needs to play sometimes to be the most productive. There was a Welsh writer named James Howell who said, "All work and no play makes Jack a dull boy." I say he wasn't talking about children. He was talking about us adults.

Play is essential for all humans, and we are going to talk about why. Before we do that, I want to take a bit of a left turn and talk about animals because we're not the only creatures that play. I know this firsthand. Almost every evening, around 6:00 p.m., my dog walks around the house holding a stuffed animal in her mouth, bumping into everyone, and trying to get them to play with her. If one person doesn't respond, she will go on to the next one. If no one responds, she will audibly sigh, drop the stuffy, and plop on her pillow dejectedly. She does this nearly every night and has done it most of her life.

Dolce and her toy.

We were in Hawaii a few years ago on a sailing boat for a cruise. In the middle of nowhere, dolphins danced through the water, playing in the wake of the boat. The ocean around us looked empty, because they weren't just jumping and spinning anywhere; they were doing it in the waves of the boat where we were. They were playing.

Crows are known to slide down roofs in the snow, then climb back up and repeat. There is no other explanation for this other than they are playing.

Almost all young hunting animals wrestle, growl, and paw at each other as infants. Like humans, they are playing to learn how to live.

Did you know that rats laugh when tickled? They actually giggle. Wow. That fact made me look at them in a whole new way, and there is going to be a future chapter just on laughter because... well, you'll have to read about that later. On the contrary, rats deprived of play struggle with problem-solving and exhibit anxiety-like behaviors.

So, animals and humans play, but they don't *just* play. They *look* for ways to play. How many times have you brought home a gift for your child that is in a big box? After you give them their gift, their immediate next question is, invariably: "Can I have the box?" Why? Their imagination is already going, and that is important to remember. Play activates the imagination. It helps us create, learn, and solve problems.

<u>"Let the Music Fill You"</u>

While a lot of my songs are about serious subjects, I also love writing about playing and having fun. A recent release is called "Let the Music Fill You." I wrote a song for Carlos Santana, and while he didn't end up playing on it, his percussionist of thirty years, Karl Perazzo, did amazingly on it.

When I was writing that song, I had imagined a scene on the streets of a Latin city where everyone spontaneously gets up, dances, and plays. It was so fun to fly to Buenos Aires, Argentina, and play in the streets of Palermo to film the music video about letting loose and playing.

Filming that music video took three or four hours while the streets were filled with people, but it felt like only a few minutes. From my perspective, that wasn't work—it was play. I think everyone, except maybe the videographers, would agree. The videographers had the hardest job, which was trying to keep too many people from coming through the shot, watching the traffic, and keeping our dancers all in line. (Thank you Mariano and Derek Dawidson.)

So... why do animals and humans play? The simplest answer is because it's fun. But why do we find it fun? At its most basic, fun things make us happy. Our brains fire off endorphins, and we create connections with our surroundings and others, much like when we laugh. Fun and play are contagious. Perhaps you've experienced this when you reluctantly joined a game—maybe flag football, a board game, or a card game. You really didn't like it at first, but once you got going, you forgot why you didn't want to play in the first place.

The "play circuits" are deep inside our brains. They're a basic part of how we're made. It is not a learned behavior, but a hardwired one. Anytime we disregard something we're hardwired for, we react poorly. Try not to drink or eat. Try going without adequate sleep. Think of how you feel when you're lonely or don't feel loved and appreciated. All those things are basic needs, and we need to include play in that list. It is a biological necessity, not an elective, and not just when we're children, but throughout our lives.

Even adults who get to do things that many consider play for their work, like professional athletes, are most productive when they *feel* like they are playing. They have more energy, are looser, and feel more engaged and relaxed. Michael Jordan was noted to have a very unusual clause in his contract. It was called the "Love of Game Clause." This clause recognized that he loved the game of basketball, not just the business, and allowed him to play whenever he wanted.

Athletes who love what they do tend to be the best at what they do. They love to play, and that freedom allows them to become their best selves. Perhaps we can all take a lesson from that.

Albert Einstein is often attributed with saying, "Play is the highest form of research" (though it's debated who actually said it). He meant that if a person was playing, they were free to explore, learn, and discover. That leads to experimentation and new ideas, which more freely happen when the mind is unburdened. They call those moments of brilliance "eureka" moments. The science behind that says those moments of brilliance come when the problem at hand isn't in your conscious thoughts.

In other words, you're not working. Your mind is playing, creating, and imagining. A 2014 Frontiers in Psychology study found that play increases neuroplasticity, making us more adaptable and quick-thinking. That makes sense because play, by definition, does not have a preplanned path or outcome. So when we play, we're always adapting and changing our thinking. Take, for instance, the game of hide-and-seek. Now, that game is really just an advanced game of "peekaboo," but it requires a lot of different kinds of thinking, planning, and strategies that are essential to learn as children. Or, for that matter, to remember as adults.

Think of all that is happening during that game from the perspective of those involved. Child's Play in Action talks about fourteen different things a child or adult goes through in that game.

Number one: Working memory. You have to remember the rules. Are you hiding or seeking? Where can you go, and what is off limits—

perhaps your parents' bedroom?

Number two: Task initiation. You have to strategize the best place to hide. Is that spot too close to the seeker or too far away? Is it in plain sight or hidden?

Number three: Organization. If you are the seeker, you have to remember where you've already looked.

Number four: Planning. When you find the perfect spot, do you fit?

Number five: Perspective. You often ask yourself, "If I were the seeker, where would I look first?"

Number six: Flexible thinking. "OK, they weren't where I thought they would be. So now where do I look?"

Number seven: Impulse control. Someone is getting really close— if you start giggling, it would show a lack of impulse control.

Number eight: Emotional control. You can't get mad just because someone else is really good at the game. It is just a game.

Number nine: Boosting happiness. Both hiding and seeking are fun. When you find a person or are found, there is generally a little celebration.

Number ten: Work through separations. You learn that just because your mom hid from you doesn't mean she is gone forever.

Number eleven: Courage. Sometimes you need to hide in a dark spot, or somewhere there could be something scary, like spiders. Or worse, your brother.

Number twelve: Independence. One of the rules is that you have to make your own decisions because if someone helps you, then they know where you're hidden.

Number thirteen: Physicality. Figuring out how to fit under the kitchen sink may take some extraordinary contortions.

Number fourteen: Exercise. It will get your heartbeat going.

All fourteen of these things are going on, all in the simple game of hide and seek. Other games, like basketball, Monopoly, or Uno, are more complicated (my family is playing a lot of Uno Flex right now). Playing games constantly challenges us to adapt, or at least, change our thinking, strategize, and even improve our health.

Notice that playing makes us both smarter and healthier. If you were selling a pill that was guaranteed to make us smarter and healthier, we would be lining up for it. If someone said that doing something fun for a few minutes a day was guaranteed to make everyone happier, smarter, and healthier, it'd be easy to think we would all be volunteering for it. That is what play does. It's kind of strange that oftentimes we turn our play into work. I recently had this conversation with a friend who plays the cello. She has become really, really good. GRAMMY®-winning good. When people started praising her, her parents enrolled her in a school and hired private tutors. She practiced hard, became even better, and started doing professional sessions. Now she is quite famous. Somewhere along the line, however, the playing turned into work, so much so that she has considered quitting. If you asked her why, I think she would say, "Because it is no longer fun."

We do that with all kinds of gifts that we see in people, from drawing to singing to math. We often forget that what makes a person really good at something is often the fact that it is done for fun and play, not because it is required of them. Sometimes a hobby should just stay a hobby because once it turns into work, it loses that play factor. It starts to feel like a responsibility, and instead of bringing joy into our lives, it brings responsibility.

"We don't stop playing because we grow old, we grow old because we stop playing." That was said by George Barnard Shaw, but it is a truism. When we stop playing, we literally age. Why?

Play reduces cortisol, the stress hormone, and releases endorphins, making us feel younger. Play makes us more active, increasing our life satisfaction and physical health. Active physical play builds our immune systems. It forms friendships and connections, plus fosters trust and learned cooperation. The Harvard Study of Adult Development, in one of the longest-running studies on happiness, found that playful relationships correlate with longevity and fulfillment. So, in a very literal way, we grow old because we stop playing. I don't know about you, but I'm tired of growing old, so I intend to play more.

So, the question comes up: is every kind of play beneficial to us? The answer is no. Some play is actually detrimental to us as humans, especially young humans. Certain types of play make us impatient, impulsive, and inhibit our ability to empathize with others. It can hinder our natural instinct and our need to form bonds with humans, animals, and our earth. That kind of play sounds really unhealthy, doesn't it?

Patricia Kuhl is one of the world's leading brain scientists. Here is what she says about this kind of play: "What we've discovered is that little babies, under a year old, do not learn from a machine. *Even if you show them captivating videos,* the difference in learning is extraordinary. You get genius learning from a live human being, and you get *zero learning* from a machine."

ZERO learning from a machine or electronic devices for infants and young children. For children to grow up and learn, for them to be patient, creative, and productive, they need to learn to focus and let their imagination grow. They require stimulus from the environments around them. And very importantly, they need time to process all those words and things they see. The voices they hear and the faces they study.

Screens are designed to grab and keep attention, not to help us grow. They feed us what they are serving, not what we need. When children spend too much time with these highly engaging apps and games, everything is immediate—instant gratification. Face-to-face interactions are the only way young children learn how to read and understand nonverbal communication. In a revealing 2014 UCLA study, researchers found that children who spent five days without screens in a nature camp significantly improved their ability to read facial expressions and emotions compared to those who continued regular screen use.

When you read a storybook to a child, their entire body, focus, and, more importantly, brain, is creating worlds and understanding. They're imagining, anticipating, and daydreaming. That does not happen if they play with screens, simply because the stories are too fast, too flashy, and too easy to swipe away. They're overstimulating, which is addictive, but not beneficial.

If young children are constantly being stimulated by screens, they forget how to rely on themselves or others for entertainment. This leads to frustration, hinders imagination and motivation, and makes them hyperactive because their minds and bodies are used to constant stimulation.

A 2018 study of pediatrics found that children who engage in real-world play show significantly higher problem-solving skills and emotional intelligence than those with high screen exposure. Try this test: give your child a cardboard box, some strings, and some paper, and see what they come up with. Maybe a rocket ship, a castle, a time machine? If they haven't done this in a while, give them time. Don't give up. Children will find a way to play with the world around them, and this is good and helps them grow.

In addition to all the emotional and mental benefits of playing with real-life things rather than screens, physical activities help them develop fine motor skills. You might think that developing motor skills is one of the few benefits of screens, but that is incorrect. They lead to weaker fine motor skills because swiping and tapping do not provide the same sensory feedback and hand-eye coordination that playing with a ball or making a fort in the sand does.

In addition, there is a measurable increase in waist size and diabetes for every additional hour of screen time. In the last study I read by Feng Lin, 43 percent of teenagers and young adults who spent an average of around three hours a day of screen time were obese, and over 8 percent had already developed type 2 diabetes in their teenage years.

The bottom line is that the kind of play matters—and not just to children. It applies to all of us, whether nine days or 109 years old. We were designed to play and have fun with each other and the world around us. We become more balanced, better adjusted, happier humans when we do that.

It is not that hard to find something to play with. As I said, even my eleven-year-old can keep herself very happy with a cardboard box for an afternoon.

When adults play, scientists see a reduction in stress levels, creativity boosts, mood improvements, and stronger connections between friends and family. The saying, "Couples that play together stay together," is true. Couples who regularly play together feel a stronger connection to each other. Ask all the people who play pickleball, and I think they would heartily agree. They might suggest not playing on the same team with your partner, but there is a tremendous connection created when couples play together.

Physical play keeps us young, keeps our minds and reflexes sharp, and helps maintain our health. Remember the quote from George

Bernard Shaw, "We don't stop playing because we grow old, we grow old because we stop playing." Let's stop growing old together and play more.

Fifteen Seconds to Change Your World

You guessed it—for this tip, we want to play. I worked hard to come up with a list of things that you can do in fifteen seconds. Now, I understand you might not be in a place where this is safe right now. So please don't do anything dangerous. Don't get fired and don't do anything that you couldn't do in front of your mother—or in front of my mother.

Here is my list:

Find something—anything—and play with it like a six-year-old. It could be a piece of paper, a pen, a paperclip, a hair tie, or a box. What do you see in that object? What could it be? Let your imagination go.

Make funny faces at someone or at yourself in the mirror. My daughter calls this game "mad faces."

Skip around or, better yet, hop on one foot in a circle.

Make funny voices. Do you do a good Donald Duck or Mickey Mouse? Go for it.

Roll down your window and bark at a dog or meow at a cat. My daughter scrunches down in her car seat when my husband does this.

This is my new favorite: Try to keep a piece of Kleenex in the air by blowing air under it. This is a really fun one that I just made up. I call it "God Save The King," but that is a whole other story for the next chapter.

My Fifteen Seconds

I played a family game called Hacky Sack dodgeball. My daughter was the moving target. My husband and I took turns throwing a hacky sack at her. She decided that if we hit her legs, we would get one point; arms, two points; and tummy, ten points. It was a lot of fun. I highly recommend all parents play this game with their kids before they're smart enough to say, "Why do I have to be the moving target?"... just don't throw it too hard!

Citations and references for this chapter are located at the end of the book.

Episode 20

Make Me Laugh

It was the smell that woke me up. It wasn't a good smell, but I knew what it was. Given that I was alone on the second floor, it meant the smell was emanating from downstairs. This was not a normal occurrence, as normally the smell was contained, and this knowledge permeated my consciousness as I walked down the stairs.

Before continuing towards the smell, I stopped at the kitchen and picked up a bag, a full roll of heavy paper towels, some gloves, and some spray cleaner. I could smell the odor even from the kitchen. That was not a good sign.

When I walked into the room, I looked into the crib with trepidation, where my daughter was supposed to be sleeping. However, I could hear that she was not. My apprehension was high as I looked over the railing. I sighed the sigh that only a parent knows. It is a mixture of resignation and conviction to just get it done.

There was poop everywhere. Story had decided that playing with a full diaper was a good idea. I strongly disagreed, and I think my opinion was shared by the bedding, the crib, and her favorite stuffed animal (who, as I write this eight years later, sits on a high bookshelf missing one foot and losing stuffing out of multiple holes… and that is after three rebuilding attempts).

To top it off, Story was delighted, limbs flying around, making getting close to the biohazard zone dangerous. My ducking and waving were out of self-preservation. However, Story thought I was now playing "peekaboo" and reacted animatedly. That was not helpful at all.

I responded louder than intended: "Stop." She froze long enough for me to grab the diaper and what remained of the poop and get it into a bag. I then ran to the bathtub, turned it on, grabbed a very delighted child, and washed her off.

With her safely away from the crib, I headed back to work on the cleanup. It seemed the initial episode had happened quite a while before, as much was dried onto the crib and required scrubbing. That explained the weird dream I had about an eerily similar scene when I thought I was happily sleeping. Turns out the DMN still works when you're asleep. Something new to Google.

With the crib cleaned and sheets and blankets in the wash, I tied the bag shut. I'm really sorry to admit this to you, but I was using a plastic bag exactly for this reason—I walked it towards the kitchen to dispose of.

I expected the smell to be dissipated by then, but strangely, it was not. So, after placing the bag into the garbage, I pulled out a can of air freshener. Now, I normally do not like the chemical smell of air fresheners. However, as a parent, you learn there are compromises to be made, and there are smells that are just better than others.

In this case, I hoped "tropical breeze" was strong enough to eradicate the other smell. I walked from the kitchen to the bedroom, holding my breath while spraying behind me all the way back to Story's room, where I quickly made sure she wasn't doing anything that would add to my angst. She was happily playing.

Relieved that the ordeal was over, I went to put away the air freshener and took a nice, deep breath, anticipating nothing but the chemically fresh smell of "tropical breeze." Unfortunately, that was not the dominant smell.

It occurred to me that I hadn't seen the dog. I walked into the living room to find Dolce sitting on the white rug, which she very well knew she was not supposed to be doing.

Seeing me, she jumped up, ran to the hallway, and looked back at me. That is when I noticed the smell emanating from behind the couch. Sure enough, the dog had pooped, likely after smelling the wonderful aroma from Story's room a few hours before.

Another resigned sigh, and I headed back to the kitchen for another plastic bag, the now half-roll of paper towels, cleaner spray, gloves, and the "tropical breeze."

I wasn't even upset anymore. It was more like "just get it done." After I cleaned it up, I noticed the dog was still acting weird, but I just chalked that up to pooping in the house. I sprayed the "tropical breeze" and brought everything back to the kitchen.

At this point, I was pretty confident I would have the smell of poop in my nose for a while longer, so it really wasn't surprising that I could still smell it. That said, it was pretty strong.

The dog appeared again and ran away. I figured I needed to do a full walkthrough and see if I missed anything. And I had. It was hidden on the far side of the dining room table. I was not happy. I even thought about just leaving it there until I was in a better mental state. Instead, I went to the kitchen for a third time, got a third plastic bag, and everything else.

It was then that I heard a sound that made my blood chill. I heard Roomba start up. That normally would not have been a cause of anxiety, but that particular Roomba was a few feet away from the dog deposit I had just seen, which was quite large (and not totally solid).

I ran into the dining room just as Roomba and the poop greeted each other—or I should say, collided. And that is when poop started flying.

If you know anything about Roombas, they have these little whisks that spin at a high RPM to grab dust. Note to manufacturer: Those little whisks are great at gathering dust but also do a commendable job on flinging wet poop a good ten feet in all directions.

I hid behind a wall, mentally picturing the devastation that was happening in the dining room, trying to figure out how I was going to stop this massacre without getting covered in poop.

It occurred to me that Story would find this really funny, and I was wondering if I could just let her try to capture it by herself. That thought quickly passed. She would have to wait unknowingly back in her crib until I told her the story five years later.

It was at that point that I heard Roomba get himself stuck between the legs of a chair, which at least meant that he wasn't free-flinging, but flinging in a limited circle.

The hastily made plan was to jump onto the dining room table, which, fortunately, was not glass. With a mad dash, I rounded the wall, stepped on a chair, and found myself in relative safety on the top of the table. I have to say, though, that the moment passed quickly as I surveyed the damage to the white walls. There were innocuous specks of brown everywhere, so much so that it looked like the painted walls had transformed into one of those artsy splattered canvases, but in a single light brown color. That is, other than the odd specks of green, which revealed what Story must have secretly fed the dog the night before.

My more pressing job was to figure out how to reach down to the Roomba, which was still pinging around the legs of the chair. I used a paper towel in one hand to shield my eyes as I tried to locate exactly where he was.

Yes, Roomba was a "he." I don't know why, but I was very unhappy with him at the moment, and I told him so in not too nice words.

From a quick glance, I was thankful, if you could call it that. He was just below me, contentedly spinning in the remnants of poop. With what I view as one of the bravest acts of my life, I quickly reached over as far as I could reach and went for the off button.

At that moment, I regretted not getting the Roomba with the remote app. I was also worried about falling off the table and landing in... Yeah, you get the picture.

But I'm very happy to report that I actually managed to stop him. It took me a couple of hours to clean up the mess, and when it was all done, Roomba and I stood over the garbage bin by the garage. The thing was, he was only about a week old and cost over $500, but I was having a very serious internal conversation about throwing him out.

I actually put him in a bag and tied him up. It wasn't worth the $500 to deal with all the nooks and crannies inside that miserable little robot. But then the cheapskate in me got the best of me.

It was honestly one of the worst jobs in my life, worse than the overflowing Honey Bucket (one of those portable plastic toilets you see at construction sites) I had to deal with when I was twenty-five, while 100 women waited to use it.

If I had to do it over again, Roomba would have met his maker that day. Instead, as life often does, I was surprised, and that Roomba still lives with us today. Once in a while, he does some really strange thing that makes me wonder about him and if the trauma of that poop episode messed with his little computer brain a little too much. But like all of us, he has been through a lot and survived, so there is that.

This story was actually my husband's, but it's one of my favorites, and I've been wanting to tell it. I hope it made you laugh because that is our topic today. We've talked about humor before, but this chapter is specifically about laughing. Why do we do it? What does it do, and how can it help us change our world? And, yes, in only fifteen seconds. I'm looking forward to showing you how it can do that.

When we laugh, all kinds of good things happen to our body and mind. We know that playing, being in love, eating, and going on nature walks release endorphins, dopamine, and serotonin. When you laugh, your body releases all three of them at the same time. That means you are carefree, feeling connected, and can suddenly be in a good mood. It is not possible to be in a bad mood while you are laughing because it is your body's way of saying, "We need to let go and just be free for a moment."

When you laugh hard, your heart rate also goes up, improving blood flow and increasing your oxygen levels, which lowers blood pressure. If you laugh a lot, it can reduce the risk of heart disease. So next time your doctor tells you to exercise more, maybe ask him if he would write a prescription for a comedy show so your insurance would cover it.

Laughter reduces pain. Have you ever stubbed your toe doing something stupid and started hopping around holding your foot and trying not to laugh? There was a study with children whose hands were placed in ice-cold water, then they were shown a funny show. When they were laughing, they didn't notice the pain nearly as much.

According to the Mayo Clinic, negative thoughts manifest as chemical reactions that can affect your body by bringing more stress into your system and decreasing your immunity. By contrast, positive thoughts can actually release neural peptides that help fight stress and potentially more serious illnesses.

So laughter literally makes you feel better, and it gives a whole new perspective on the saying "laughter is the best medicine" because it really has a beneficial physical effect on our immune system.

Lastly, laughter is a great workout. I'm sure you have laughed so hard your abs hurt. I just had this happen yesterday when we were playing our new game, "God Save the King."

It started with a story about a king who was very sick, so all his patrons came to the town square to hear the news. A herald soon appeared on the palace balcony, raised his hands, and hushed the crowd whose faces were all upturned to listen. He said, "I have good news and bad news. The bad news is that the king needs a new heart." The crowd was silent. "The good news is that we found one," he stated loudly.

Hearing that, the crowd cheered madly. He continued, "A very lucky person in the audience today will be chosen to donate his heart to the king."

There was hushed murmuring in the crowd, so the herald continued, "I'm going to drop this feather, and whoever the feather touches, God has chosen him to donate his heart to save the king."

He dropped the feather, and everyone was silent and still, watching as it slowly floated down toward a young boy. Right before it touched him, the boy yelled out, "God save the king!" and *pffffff* blew the feather toward his neighbor, who repeated the phrase "God save the king!" and *pffffff* blew the feather on to the next person, who continued the action, and on it went. Seems no one wanted to be the heart donor. When we heard that story, we decided to use Kleenex as the feather and tried to keep it in the air by—*pffffff*—blowing at it. It is hilarious, fun, and quite a workout as people dive around, trying to keep the Kleenex from hitting the ground or themselves. We even made variations where you had to use only words instead of blowing. I strongly encourage you to try this game if you haven't laughed hard in a long time.

"Make Me Smile"

This is the theme song for this podcast, called *"Make Me Smile,"* but it also talks about laughing. I hope it helps you get in the mood for the rest of this amazing discussion.

My favorite line in that song is, "Kick your shoes on the floor. Leave your worries at my door. Can we laugh for a while and make me smile?" It is my goal to have you laugh with me today.

Did you know that a good laugh engages your diaphragm, abs, and shoulders and burns up to forty calories? As a side point, yelling and

screaming also engage a lot of physical muscles, but obviously do not have the same benefit and, in fact, increase blood pressure and risk of heart attack. Would you rather be laughing or screaming?

At least one study has shown that people who were able to laugh something off, like spilling wine on their sleeve, rather than be embarrassed or angry, have fewer heart attacks. So next time you ruin your favorite sweater, maybe think about the great story you will be able to tell your spouse instead of being upset. It could work.

There are many mental and emotional benefits to laughing as well. Laughter lowers stress and relaxes your muscles. It has been shown that people who laugh often can cope with challenges positively. Remember the last time you were in an argument with your partner, and they did something funny? You started to smile and then tried to stop yourself... maybe you even said, "Stop that! I want to be mad at you."

You do that because you know that once you start smiling and laughing, you can no longer be mad. When the other person senses that opening, what do they do? They keep going because they also know the bad mood will go away if they can keep it up. It is literally impossible to be in a bad mood when you are laughing. It's like fog lifting in your brain.

In fact, your mind goes into the DMN, autopilot for the brain. Hard laughter can even cause a loss of control of your legs, your bladder, and your tears. That is why we say, "I laughed so hard I cried." In that context, the evidence of tears is a good thing.

Laughing can even override your breathing. You've experienced this when you're laughing so hard that you literally start gasping for breath. You probably said something like, "Please stop. I can't breathe."

That's your body's way of telling you that at that moment, it is having so much fun that it would rather keep laughing than breathing. Not sure if that is actually a good idea.

Did you know there is a difference between a male's and a female's laughter in relationships? Robert R. Provini, PhD, a behavioral neurobiologist at the University of Maryland in Baltimore, did a study on this. If a woman is talking to a friend, they tend to laugh, whether they are talking to a male or a female. However, if a male is talking, he is more likely to laugh if he is with other males rather than with females.

Between the sexes, the least amount of speaker laughter was when a male was talking to a female, which is contrary to what women are attracted to. Women are very attracted to men who make them laugh. They get more attracted the more they are made to laugh. Seems like a disconnect to me, but something all you guys might want to take note of.

Dr. Provini has studied laughter for over ten years. He says that laughter is the best way to understand humans because everyone laughs. Every healthy baby, teenager, adult, and senior of every nationality and culture has the ability to laugh. It is a universal language that goes beyond vocabulary and speech, and nearly every person does it the same way. That tells us something about why we laugh.

You see, we're more likely to laugh in groups rather than alone. Dr. Pravini noted that people laughed thirty times more often when they were around other people compared to being by themselves, even if they found the thing that amused them, just as funny when alone.

In another study across dozens of social lines and nearly a thousand people, when the researchers played recordings of people laughing together, the audience could tell by the laughter whether the people on the recordings were friends or had just met each other. That's amazing. It means that, while we can laugh with nearly everyone, when we laugh with our friends, it is slightly different because of our connection.

~~~~~~~~~~~~~~~

But why do we laugh? We laugh because we want to feel connected to people. To, in essence, say, "You and I are in sync here. We have a bond and an understanding, and I like that."

Well, it can be done with anyone. With friends, it draws us even closer to them. Dr. Provini observed that laughter is not about jokes. If we pay attention to everyday life, we laugh. When we do that with friends, it bonds us. It makes us feel connected.

Do you remember laughing so hard as a child that you held onto each other or leaned on each other's shoulders or backs, or even ended up on the floor rolling around? Does that memory bring a smile to your face? That is connection. That is healthy and makes us strong.
~~~~~~~~~~~~~~~

It gives us the will to overcome things together and is the opposite of loneliness. In my research on the subject, another behavior had a similar effect: grooming. When a parent grooms a child's hair, it is a bonding experience. Some women find that when their partner brushes their hair, it is very intimate, and they feel connected.

I know lots of people who love going to a salon and having their hair washed, but laughing together is probably a lot more acceptable in public than going around brushing or stroking people's hair or picking out bugs like some primates do. Speaking of which, did you know that at least sixty-five animals laugh?

Rats giggle. Dogs pant and kick their paws. Some parrots cackle. And of course, hyenas are famous for their laughter. My husband said when he saw them in the wild in Africa, it was more like a sinister laugh than a playful one. If you saw the way they hunted, you would understand. Not sure I want to see that; *The Lion King* was traumatic enough.

There are many kinds of laughter and reasons why we laugh. When someone tickles us, we laugh. Some people laugh when they're nervous. I laugh at inappropriate times when I feel uncomfortable. This causes my husband to look at me very strangely when we're watching something very serious, like a person dying of a sickness, and I start laughing. I do remind him that I don't find it funny, but I think he finds it disconcerting. I get it. Sorry.

Then there are the cackles or chortles. My personal favorite is the snort. Do you know someone who, when they laugh uncontrollably, they snort? Of course, when everyone hears a snort, it makes everyone laugh harder. Just remember that it is a good thing.

Have you ever tried a fake snort laugh? You can't do it. A snort means that something is truly deeply funny to that person. But you can fake laugh. You could pretend by saying, "Ha ha ha ha ha!" Right? But humans—and I think animals—can always tell. Real laughter is spontaneous and involves our whole bodies, while fake laughter is just our mouth articulating the sound.

UCLA communication researcher Greg Bryant says everyone can tell a fake laugh, and the reason is quite simple. Fake laughter sounds more like speech, while real laughter has distinct acoustic features like higher pitch, a faster burst of non-articulated sounds, and more non-tonal noise. Genuine laughs are produced by an emotional vocal system, while fake laughs are produced by a speech system, which is distinct.

That doesn't mean that fake laughter isn't good for us. In fact, sometimes fake laughing will cause a person and others to laugh. There is a whole group of YouTube videos about fake laughing because it's funny. Kim McIntyre, a laughter club leader at the Getting Well campus in Orlando, says, "Ninety percent of the time, when we start out with forced laughter, people start laughing. Pretty soon, there's an overwhelming amount of genuine laughter. Your ear hears it, and you start laughing." Then she says to try this next step: Turn the corners of your mouth up into a smile and then give a laugh, even if it feels forced. Observe how that made you feel. Are your muscles a little less tense? Do you feel more relaxed or buoyant? Isn't that just wonderful? Humans are such complex creatures who want to play so much that we will even fake it until they make it.

Laughter is also very individual. My husband tells the story of traveling to another state and watching a movie in a theater. During a particular scene, he started laughing out loud, at which someone about three rows in front of him turned around and said his name in the form of a question. It was a friend that he hadn't seen in years. They recognized his laugh.

This is called a "laugh print," a personal signature that belongs only to us. This is so unique that the company Sun Chips ran a campaign where consumers could share their laugh print online.

I love it, and I love Sun Chips. What I found endearing is that my husband's friends knew his laugh print. I think it would be great to ask ourselves if the people around us know ours. If they don't, perhaps it is time that they did, as there is no better way to form lasting connections than by laughing together. In the world we live in today, a little more laughter couldn't hurt.

A Catholic monk named Benedict tried to tell his monks not to laugh 1,500 years ago. There was a whole movie about it called The Name of the Rose. But not laughing is not life. Not laughing is depressing and sad, and the world is sad enough.

Let's remember that laughing is a choice. We can choose to find something funny, or we can get angry about it. We can choose to be silly and help the people around us laugh. By doing so, perhaps we will alleviate a little of their stress and burden and bring them closer to us. A community that laughs together is connected, and that connection is what makes us well human.

This is the simplest one I think you're going to hear from me, as it requires you to only listen.

Scan the QR code below to listen to and watch this video clip:

That clip was from a news program, RTV Noord. Those two never did get their composure back, but isn't that great? How did that make you feel? Do you feel happy, more relaxed? While you were listening to those two, were you thinking about all the work that awaits you?

So, our fifteen-second action today is simply to find time to laugh, at least one time today. We can find that anywhere in the world around us. We have to just decide to look for it.

Citations and references for this chapter are located at the end of the book.

Living Without Fear

I fear being left. I know where it came from. When I was five, my parents dropped me off at a boarding school and left. My father never returned. I know it is not a logical fear—just because my parents did that to me does not mean that the rest of the people in my life will do that.

But when it came to my fear, logic didn't matter. The understanding and reassurance of others didn't matter. That fear became the dominant relationship force in my life. If I felt I was getting too close to a friend, I would leave. If my boyfriend wanted to be closer to me, I would leave. If a challenge arose in a relationship, I would leave. Fear caused me and others so much unnecessary pain. I wanted—no, I *needed*—to change that.

Originally, fear was hardwired into us to save us from danger. Stay away from cliffs, beware of fire, sharp objects, and other dangers. Run into a mean person or animal? Our brain's fear center would set alarms off, and we would literally, figuratively, or mentally leave to save ourselves from pain, whether physical or emotional.

Somewhere along the line, fear became the reason and not the explanation. We are afraid of failure, so we don't try. It wasn't that we were afraid of the new job. We became afraid of failing at the new job. Fear became the reason why we stopped doing things.

The COVID outbreak certainly didn't help. Fear took over the world; whether it was real or imagined didn't matter. Fear dictated almost everything we did for over three years. People stopped traveling, getting together, laughing together, and smiling at strangers. Fear made us stop living.

We started even fearing the beautiful things in life, like a hug. It is no wonder that anxiety, depression, and stress all increased during those times, and they still remain high.

The problem was the boogeyman syndrome (this is my name for it, not a real one). You see, the boogeyman lived under the bed or in the basement. At least, that is what we imagined, but it wasn't a real boogeyman. It was a fear of the unknown, just like when I was three and wondering what was under the bed. I didn't know for sure. What was in the basement? I didn't know. It became a fear of the unknown.

Once we are in its grip, the fear of the unknown is almost impossible to overcome because, by definition, it is unknown. Former U.S. President Franklin D. Roosevelt famously said, "The only thing to fear is fear itself." He said this during an incredibly difficult economic time (the Great Depression), and what he meant was that the fear of what *might* happen was creating a spiral effect where no one believed in anything. In other words, fear of the boogeyman was the danger because everyone talked about, was worried about, and was certain that the boogeyman was going to appear.

Of course, the only figurative boogeyman was in the collective mind of the world. By providing people with vision and confidence, the boogeyman became just that: a fictional character that only existed and had power if we gave him power.

In 1933, changing the mindset of fear to confidence and hope altered the course of the world. However, fear has the same effect, but it alters the world in a negative way.

Think of all the things it can impact. Fear stops us from exploring because we are not positive about what is around the corner. Fear stops us from trying new things because we might fail. Fear stops us from having adventures because there might be dangers lurking. Fear of losing control, losing someone you love, fear of other people's opinions of success, fear of being triggered, fear of embarrassment...

Are we starting to get the idea that fear can stop us from actually living? It can. It did for me. Did I want it to? No, but it wasn't a conscious decision that I made. It came from much deeper.

It's not only mental. Fear presents itself in physical ways. Your heart races, palms sweat, and your body tenses. Maybe that knot in your back starts hurting. Your breath shortens. Fear can literally paralyze us. Living in fear is not really living. It is surviving. If you ask anyone on Earth, "Would you rather live or just survive?" you will get a resounding answer, "We want to live." Don't you?

So, understanding how fear molds our lives and shapes our attitudes and decisions can help us take back our lives and not be afraid of fear itself. Or, at least, to only fear things that really should be feared, like that eleven-foot brown bear on its hind legs roaring in front of us.

We all can mentally acknowledge that fearing something just because it is unknown makes little sense. Yet many of us live our lives by unseen decisions. For instance, we might find ourselves in the same bad relationship with the same unhealthy personality, yet we do it over and over. When we are stressed, we might revert to bad habits like eating badly or addictions. It's almost as if an unseen thing is controlling us, and many times that is exactly what it is. An unseen fear.

We're going to take an in-depth look at fear, so we can recognize whether fear is keeping us in survival mode and, if it is, find a way to put it back in its proper place, taking back our humanity and lives.

When we face perceived danger, we enter fight or flight mode. The body triggers the release of adrenaline and cortisol, making us ready to run like the wind or, if we can't, to fight. In this mindset, there is little rational thought. It is all reaction. You've heard of the mother who lifted a car off her infant after a car crash. That is not rational thought. It is adrenaline and cortisol. It even has a term: "Hysterical strength."

Wikipedia defines it this way: "Hysterical strength is a display of extreme physical strength by humans, beyond what is believed to be within their capacity, usually occurring when people are in—or perceive themselves, or others, to be—life-or-death situations." The body and mind go on automatically. But what if we lived our lives always filled with adrenaline and cortisol?

Did you know that procrastination can create adrenaline? Have you ever met someone who seems to live from crisis to crisis? Perhaps the soldier who has post-traumatic stress disorder, but only feels comfortable in the panic of war? Living in these kinds of situations can create a cortisol or adrenaline addiction, where we subconsciously look for high-stress situations because that is what we have become accustomed to. It is the same with fear. As Franklin D. Roosevelt said in 1933, the entire nation was gripped by fear, and they made decisions not on rational thought, but on the idea that imminent doom was approaching. They were caught in a loop of fear.

As I experienced personally, we can get caught in a loop of fear without even realizing it. I certainly didn't want to be there, but it had a very real effect on me and those around me. Again, we have to realize that fear, by definition, is not reasoning. The amygdala, the part of our brain that controls fear, overrides rational thinking and instead makes decisions on emotion instead of logic. Think of the last time a purely emotional decision worked out well for you, and then you begin to understand the danger of letting the amygdala make your life decisions.

Fear causes a reaction, not a conscious thought. That is important to remember. What we do because we are fearful is simply a reaction, like how you move when your funny bone is hit accidentally. We even do this intentionally because it can be exhilarating. On top of the Stratosphere in Las Vegas, there was a rollercoaster and a Big Shot ride. I went on the Big Shot. It was so terrifying that there were warning signs all along the ticket line: those with weak hearts or other physical ailments were warned multiple times. You were also required to empty your pockets and remove your shoes. The rides are designed to cause maximum fear, and people lined up to do so intentionally, as did I. My husband wisely refused, despite the peer pressure we put on him.

People often go to places to get scared, and this is the strange part: We know we're going to get scared, yet we still get scared. We still feel the fear and adrenaline coursing through our bodies. That is because fear is a reflex, and it happens even if we don't want it to. In that, we learn something. When we act by fear, we're acting by reflex. We're not doing what is necessarily best for us in the moment, nor in the long term. Yet one of the most basic actions we try to teach our children is to think before acting. We may very well tell them that while we ourselves might simply be repeatedly reacting to our own past fears.

Several of my friends keep trying new things. On the outside, it would seem that they just have lots of interests. They take up a new hobby, job, or class. Then, nearly every time, they quit right before finishing or before accomplishing too much. Do you know someone like that? They seem to be excited for some new adventure in life, then quit right before the finish line. That often stems from the fear of failure. Subconsciously, if they quit before they actually have to put what they have learned into practice, whether that is becoming an attorney or making a cake, they will not have failed because they never tried. That is a life being controlled by fear. The feeling of accomplishment can be very satisfying, whether that is from simply making that cake or something as big as finishing a multi-year project, but if fear never allows us to finish, we will never experience that sense of accomplishment.

Lack of self-worth often presents as fear. If a person has low self-worth, they hear criticism or suggestions as a verdict on their personal value instead of on the action or work they're doing. "Could you redo this presentation?" is interpreted as "You can't do anything right and are of no value to me."

When that fear of someone questioning our worth or value is always imminent, like a train barreling down the tracks, we react with fear as if it's a real train. It can stop us from even trying or cause us to overreact. Our reaction is not logical. It is a reflex of what we perceive as a threat to our very reason for being alive—our perceived value. That is what fear can do. It makes us want to give up trying or attack others because we are afraid we will hear the words "You are worthless," even if only in our own minds.

Fear can stop us from experiencing love. Love requires a complete giving of oneself to another person. It requires a loss of control because, in the end, you cannot control the feelings of another person. The feeling of love is the greatest emotion a human can experience, but the feeling of losing control is one of the most disconcerting feelings. It can be confusing, like falling through the air while being held in a warm embrace. That is both confusing and hugely compelling. The fear of losing control can completely stop us from experiencing that. From an emotional richness standpoint, what a tremendous loss that would be.

It is estimated that over 67 percent of all songs are written about love, but how sad would it be if we were so fearful of losing control that we rob ourselves of that perfect euphoric experience? Part of the creation of fear in our world is that we are told over and over again that we cannot rely on anyone but ourselves. We cannot trust anyone but ourselves. If that is true, then love in its purest form can never exist, and we will never experience it.

I choose not to believe that because, as the famous song "Nature Boy" by Nat King Cole says, loving someone and being loved is the greatest thing we will ever experience. It is the most basic human need.

One of my recent fears was that my songwriting and singing were not good enough and would never be good enough. That could have stopped me from going any further than my living room with my music. Instead, I kept meeting people who support me and believe in me, people who have known music for decades. Their belief in me is slowly dissipating my fears.

"I'm Not Afraid to Dream Again"

One of the first songs I wrote for Narada Michael Walden was to express this. It was a song dedicated to him entitled "I'm Not Afraid to Dream Again." I hope you enjoy listening to it.

I love that song for what it represents: me believing, seeing a dream, and not being afraid to reach for it.

Strangely, success can have its own fears if we let it. Once you taste success, you can fear losing it or fear not being able to replicate it. I think of all those so-called musical "one-hit wonders." You find yourself on top of the world, but then you start noticing how high you are, and that fear can paralyze you. It can get into our heads so much that we subconsciously sabotage ourselves.

Part of this fear is the idea that if we succeed, our value is only maintained at those dizzying heights. In reality, what if we viewed success as something that passes, like a specific time in our lives to experience? The birth of our children only happens once, but the memories and relationships stay with us forever.

It is the same with success. Instead of fearing that we cannot stay on top of the mountain, perhaps we should view it as an amazing trip up the mountain. Enjoy the view, then continue on our life journey instead of getting fixated on trying to build a castle at the top of that mountain. After all, "Who Let the Dogs Out?" was a huge one-hit wonder, and it's still a great song.

I have another particular fear that I'm not sure is very common, but I'm going to share it because it can and does affect my life. I fear being triggered. Being triggered is a post-traumatic stress disorder (PTSD) response to something I perceive happening. So, if I get a side look from my daughter or my mom says something unkind, fear takes over, freezing my ability to make rational decisions. I shut down.

I've talked about my ability to daydream. I do that even to this day when I see signs of a confrontation happening that is going to make me anxious. Please note that I'm saying the event hasn't actually happened. I only see the possibility of it happening. My fear response is to shut down and go into my own world of self-protection. When I do that, I withdraw my love from those I care most about. It is done ostensibly, out of self-preservation, but it has a negative effect on others, and being in that anxious space doesn't feel good to me. The fear of being triggered can be debilitating to me.

Perhaps you felt the inkling of this if you have a hard-to-please boss or perhaps a parent or spouse who can be harsh at times, and you hear the rise in volume of their voice or hard footsteps walking toward your door. Does that trigger you to shut down, get ready to fight, or run away? That is a fear response, not necessarily a logical one.

A writer on Medium had this insightful thought about situations like these: "To do this, take some time away from your situation and think about what's really going on—what is causing you stress? What are your concerns about this situation? Are there things that can be done to alleviate those concerns? If so, what are they? Is there anything else that could be done? Take some time to work through these issues before you make any decisions about how best to proceed." Instead of just reacting, we can calm the amygdala part of our brain and allow ourselves to use rational thought. I think you would agree that 99 percent of the time, using logical and rational thinking is better than just reacting in the same old way we always have.

~~~~~~~~~~~~~~~~
~~~~~~~~~~~~~~~~

Whatever your fear is, is that fear affecting the way you live your life? Then the goal today is to understand what is causing that fear and then break the cycle. If fear is stopping you from finishing a project, decide that you're not going to allow fear of the future to stop you. Decide that whatever happens after you complete it does not define your value.

Is fear stopping you from trying to be a singer, dancer, or street artist? Ask yourself if giving up on your dreams should really be dictated by something you're only imagining might happen or by embarrassment that you might feel. Instead, focus on the feeling of doing what you love and bringing smiles to the people who appreciate that you are living without fear.

Try to remember how you feel when you see someone living without fear. That person who dances in public. The woman or man who, late in life, decides to become something new or finish something interrupted decades before.

In this world, there are plenty of things to really be afraid of. Let's not fear things that could possibly, might, or maybe happen in the future. Let's be determined to live our lives without fear and with the intention of being who we truly are, doing what we dream of, and doing what we were made for.

~~~~~~~~~~~~~~~

Recently, my daughter, who has always been goofy and silly, is now worried about being embarrassed. She is one of the best natural dancers I've ever seen, but suddenly she won't dance in front of people. The fear of embarrassment makes her enjoy life less, and I struggle to
~~~~~~~~~~~~~~~

find a way to help her overcome this. It was, in part, the reason that I added the "be silly" fifteen-second action to my Kindness Kube™. She used to be silly all the time, and it was not only hilarious for us, but it made her happy. Now she has this fear of embarrassment that stops her from enjoying herself as much. I find that sad. That realization comes from the point that I, too, try to be too perfect in front of others.

We, as a family, now try to be less concerned about doing embarrassing things because, in reality, doing those things makes not only us happy, but those around us. Most of the actions we view as embarrassing these days actually aren't or shouldn't be. They're just not social norms anymore. Dancing, acting silly in public, laughing, or goofing off around strangers may not be acceptable, but they certainly do not hurt anyone. In fact, they will often bring a moment of happiness to everyone around us. So I say this: the fear of embarrassment needs to go away, because we would all be happier without worrying so much about what people think. Honestly, people are not thinking about us anyway. We are just not that important to them.

Oftentimes, the things we love the most as children become the things we shy away from as adults: that beat-up stuffed animal, hugs and kisses from our parents, being tickled by our siblings, or turning the music up loud and dancing like the world was blind—these are things we truly love and that make us feel like we are alive. But fear of acting childish or sentimental or showing love can cause us to relegate such important memories to the past.

Speaking of love, love can strangely create fear once you find it.

There is a poem I read a while ago, "I'm Afraid of Dying," that I wanted to share. It is from one of my favorite authors, Andrea Peters.

I'm afraid of dying.
I used to stand upon tall ladders
And look down to the depths below
Wondering what all the fuss was
If I should fall.

My mother said, "Get down!"
My brother just cried,
While I stood on the very highest step
Where the words
"No Step" reside.

I didn't conceive what was at risk,
I thought it was just life
And life wasn't that big of a deal
At least not to me.

I used to walk across high bridges
And ponder what it would be to fly
To soar for a moment or two.
If I should stumble.

My eyes must have deceived me as
Many a stranger paused
To watch,
Me. Watch the water.
The swirls, which mesmerized my mind.

I didn't give it much thought,
The fall that is
As it would end in darkness
A lack of light
And I would know nothing. Anymore.
I used to drive my car
At night
And wonder what it would be like to cross that line.
The white one.
On the side.

What it would be like to fall asleep and sail,
For a second or two,
To never know what happened.
To never awake.

It really didn't worry me that much
It only meant no more thoughts,
No more strain
Of life. Only rest.

But now I stand upon the lowest rung,
I walk along the shortest bridge,
And drive the most deserted roads
In fear.

For now, I find myself afraid to die.
Terrified of no thought.
Fearful of no consciousness.
Scared of the most timid danger.

For now, I finally know what it means to live.

For today, I met you.

When we fall in love, and that means with anyone—our children, our mates, our best friend—our life can suddenly feel so much more valuable that it can create fear in us, but this fear is actually a good fear. It holds us back from doing foolish things because we have so much to lose and don't want to lose it. That is a proper and good fear.

There are other proper fears: They include physical dangers, emotional threats, or the mental danger from abusive relationships. Financial fear requires proper and wise planning for the future. Fear of disease may help us exercise, eat better, stop bad habits, and improve our hygiene. We should fear the abuse of power. Studying the history of leaders, such as Adolf Hitler, can make us worry about unchecked power because, well, there has never been a person with unchecked power who was not eventually corrupted by it. That lesson presents proper fear.

However, the media and commercial world use fear to sell us things. Have you ever watched a commercial about a drug or a cure for a disease you never heard of? Have you ever wondered if that company was just creating fear so they could sell us something? You can buy a bomb shelter and food that lasts for twenty-five years in a bucket. I have one in my own garage because someone sold it to me.

When we feel anxious while someone is trying to sell us something, we need to stop and think about why we feel compelled to buy it. We need to learn to distinguish between that literal eleven-foot brown bear in front of us and that imagined twenty-foot brown bear hiding around the corner.

For all of humanity's history, people have manipulated or created fears in order for a particular person to be able to rise up and say, "I can keep you safe." Companies do it. Hitler did it. Julius Caesar did it. Why do they do it? Because it helps them achieve power and money. In the end, it almost never helps the people who simply react and follow. They know what we don't. When we're in a state of fear, we do what we need to feel safe, even if that might be bad for us in the long run.

"We don't think of buying a traditional Oreo as a way to bring control into our life, but that's apparently how people are behaving," said marketing professor Gregory Carpenter. They go to what they know, even if it is bad for them.

As an article by Northwestern University observed,

This spring, as COVID-19 infections spread across the country, consumers began making noticeably different choices. Shoppers stripped grocery-store shelves of household staples. Hand sanitizer sold out quickly. And consumers began buying more natural and organic foods, apparently placing healthfulness over price. At the same time, however, consumers made plenty of choices that weren't that healthy at all. They purchased dramatically more fallen-out-of-favor brands like Oreo, Doritos, and Campbell's soup. And consumers developed a renewed hankering for Big Macs and other fast-food favorites.

Fear does not make us act logically. We react to emotion.

In Frank Herbert's novel, Dune, there is a quote about fear: "I must not fear. Fear is the mind-killer. Fear is the little death that brings total obliteration. I will face my fear. I will permit it to pass over me and through me. And when it has gone past, I will turn the inner eye to see its path."

In other words, we must learn not to just react but understand our fears and what those fears make us do. Remember, there is such a thing as healthy fear. When the eleven-foot brown bear literally is standing in front of us, when we're driving on an icy road or standing near a sheer cliff, that is proper fear. We want heightened senses. We want to back off and be cautious. We want our body to be at full attention.

Then there are those other fears, those imagined fears, the boogeyman downstairs... the events we think we can foretell, but we really can't. Those fears can make us miss out on living a beautiful life, and we can find ourselves instead living in fear—fear of relationships, embarrassment, success or failure, and fear of love. Those fears are unhealthy and are mental poison.

Let's take back our freedom to choose the life we decide to live, to enjoy the beauty of friendship and love, to indulge in the journey to our success in whatever form that takes, to bake a cake and eat it, too.

Fifteen Seconds to Change Your World

This one sounds easy, but it is not. In fact, we tried it at dinner after this was written, and all of us found this challenging. While reading this episode, what fear did you think of about yourself or your life? Is it the fear of not being loved or not finding love? Ending up alone, not being valued, or dying? Whatever it is, we're going to verbalize that fear because, when we say it out loud, we may find it doesn't sound so scary after all, or the fear may not be as big as it sounds in our head. It's like taking a pin to a balloon. I'm hoping that speaking of fear deflates some of its power over us.

My Fifteen Seconds

My answer to that question was, "I'm afraid of being rejected or not being valued by the people I love. I'm afraid of being triggered and hurting the feelings of the people I love."

I guess it's not as scary as it sounded in my head.

Citations and references for this chapter are located at the end of the book.

Let's Just Dance!

"Dance like no one is watching." The first time I saw that quote, it was on a baby's onesie. I thought to myself, "Does a six-month-old really need to know that?"

Well, it turns out, they don't. At five months old, babies inherently start dancing to songs and rhythms. Babies are born to dance. When they dance—and when we dance—we smile. We're happier. We laugh more, feel more connected, and are healthier. That phrase, "Dance like no one is watching," has become more of a life mantra than a suggestion to literally dance. It has become a metaphor for pursuing happiness and experiencing unabashed joy without embarrassment, free and unbound by the stresses and anxiety of living in these difficult times. This is especially needed in our world, where it is acceptable to say horrible things to strangers online and criticize other people's opinions to the point that we claim they are inhuman because they believe differently from us.

Dancing like no one is watching casts off those limits and just lets us be human. In essence, it is saying, "Let's be ourselves. Let me be myself, and I'll let you be yourself, and let's all dance." It is an optimistic outlook, one that a jaded world would frown on and say is impossible. But is it really? What if our mindset were "Let's just dance"? Would it change the way you live?

Since many cultures do not find public dance acceptable, we instead tune in to watch other people dance. *Dancing with the Stars* has been one of the most successful TV shows of all time. It has spawned dozens of copycat shows around the world because we like to see people free from the constraints of social norms and just letting go. It's just beautiful to see humans move to music.

Instead of dancing just for fun, we created the concept of dancing for exercise because that is more acceptable. Someone figured out that dancing improves muscle strength, trains coordination, and makes us more flexible. It can also alleviate depression and stress. Amazingly, it increases the number of cells in the hippocampus, where our memory and navigation reside, showing it to be an effective treatment for diseases such as Alzheimer's. It is like a miracle drug.

So, what we had been doing for free for thousands of years started to be sold as the key to staying young and fit, and thus was born Jazzercise, Zumba, and many other pay-to-dance studios that allow you to dance with abandon under the socially acceptable guise of exercise. But watching people dance on a show or even dancing for exercise in a studio is no substitute for letting go in the privacy of our kitchens or bedrooms, is it?

Letting go completely and dancing with abandon is a feeling like no other. From a physiological standpoint, it is a unique experience. It is similar to laughing, but it adds a feeling of euphoria. That euphoria calms our minds and bodies, allowing us to float, twist, and turn without a care. This, in turn, provides amazing physical exercise along with endorphins that make us feel really good.

How many times have you danced and felt unhappy afterwards? Dancing is a mood-altering activity that alleviates stress and tension, calms us, and can be done anytime, anywhere. Animals know this inherently as well. If you have ever watched the documentary *The Planet Earth* or a similar series, you will see an abundance of birds that dance. They have exacting footwork, wing movements, and they even throw in a bit of songwriting.

Bees dance to communicate about food. Dolphins spin, leap, and do synchronized swimming. Peacocks use their amazing feathers along with dance movements. Flamingos do group dances that look like rhythmic dancing. Even elephants dance. While my dog doesn't dance, she does love music. When my husband plays the piano, she always lies down under it to listen. Many dogs are known to move with music. Dance is a part of our natural world. Amazingly, we, as humans, can appreciate the dance of all those other creatures. It makes us smile, laugh, and feel free. Doesn't seem like that was an accident, does it?

So, what is dance? Simply put, it is when our bodies move in time to music. But how does your body know what beat or rhythm comes next? Think about that. If our bodies couldn't anticipate the next rhythm, we'd always be out of sync, and dance would look completely random and uncoordinated, kind of like those wind dancing balloons at car dealerships that I've talked about.

The definition of dance is the opposite of that chaotic movement. When we think of dance, we think of coordinated movement along with the rhythm. Let's do a couple of examples. As I play these clips, notice how your body moves, even if you've never heard the song before.

"Let the Music Fill You"

The first piece is a song on a Latin beat written for Carlos Santana, called "Let the Music Fill You." Carlos didn't end up playing on it, but Karl Perrazzo, his percussionist of thirty years, is the featured artist. I hope you enjoy it.

"Move Your Body Slowly"

The second one has more of a dance beat. It was produced by Narada Michael Walden, who is famous for this kind of beat. It's called "Move Your Body Slowly."

Was your body able to anticipate the beat and dance to it? Keep a rhythm? How can it do that? How does it know what the music is going to do, even if you've never heard the song before?

It turns out there are several things at work in our brains when we dance to music. We have mirror neurons built into our brains. These mirror neurons become active when we see and hear other people doing something. Maybe you've experienced this by having the urge to play air guitar when seeing a famous guitar player riff on their instrument, or, if your friend yawns, you end up yawning.

Those are your mirror neurons at work. Well, those neurons also help you engage with the experience of music. It creates a bond between you and musical artists, and in that way, we imitate the emotions and feelings of the artist or their song.

When multiple people do this at the same time, our brains mirror each other's behaviors, and we bond not only with the music but also with the other people with whom we are mirroring.

Frontiers talks about how most music has regular beats, both stressed and unstressed. Think prominent drums, a melodic guitar, or a piano. In my song, "Let the Music Fill You," there is more guitar. "Move Your Body Slowly" was more of a drum beat.

When music has a regular beat, it makes us want to move our bodies in time with it. It's called rhythmic entrainment. In 1666, a physicist named Christian Huygens put two pendulums next to each other and started them swinging at different times. Shortly, they synchronized by themselves. That is rhythmic entrainment, but it also happens in humans when we dance. Our bodies and minds mirror what is happening with the musician and other dancers, then sync up on their own to match the musical meter.

Of course, this all happens without us thinking about it, but we can see and feel it on the dance floor or when watching dance shows. That synchronization creates an amazing, unique feeling of bonding with a group of independent minds who are feeling and moving in the same rhythm.

However, it is not only the rhythm we sync with. We also start mirroring the emotions and feelings of others in the room. Thus, playing happy music makes everyone happy. Play heavy metal, and people start shaking their heads. Play a country song, and people start swaying. Salsa? Wow, people want to salsa!

We do all of this in sync, with the same emotions, and at the same time, which creates a deep sense of belonging. Dancing one-on-one with a partner can even be more powerful. Dances that require touch, like salsa, tango, and ballroom dancing, all require incredible trust. Because of that, a deep connection, romantic and otherwise, is often formed. Dancers do not change partners often. In fact, most professional dancers change only when they must because dance partners in these types of dances grow incredibly close.

It's not just the footwork and the physical trust, but the temperament and emotions that bond partners together. They feel the same emotions at the same time and rely on each other without hesitation. That is a potent drug that can form a lifelong bond.

Then there is ballet, a genre in itself. It is the one form of dancing that most people will never personally do, but that evokes a distinct mental image—not just of tutus and skin-tight leotards, but of the bodies and athleticism. Ballet can be considered both a dance and a sport. Picture in your mind what a ballet body looks like.

Now, that is not necessarily always true, as all types of bodies can do ballet. However, there is a reason why we have a mental image of what ballet dancers look like. It requires levels of strength and agility that take years of dedication and training, and affects those dancers daily, not only while dancing.

A ballet dancer is known for their posture and flexibility. Ballet dancing incorporates full-body cardiovascular training as well as resistance training. Even National Football League (NFL) players sometimes do ballet because of the intensity of the workout. However, ballet is often not directly connected to music. It may not have a strong rhythm or beat. When you're watching it, you don't get the foot tapping and head nodding that you do with other dance music. So not all dances *must* cause these reactions.

Remember that dancing is, at its most basic, a way for people to connect. People who love ballet, both those who watch it and those who participate, have an intense love and devotion to it. It's a community and sense of belonging, the same as other forms of dance.

Likewise, some performance or drama dances are not meant to get you tapping your feet, but to elicit strong emotions and body movements from both individuals and groups. Think of a contemporary dance where the dancers present a story or convey a message without speaking. They can do that through dance.

Dance is not restricted to feeling, a beat, or bobbing our heads. It can be just a way to express emotion or elicit feelings. When we do that in a group, we're connected, which releases endorphins and makes us happy even if the story is sad. That is the way we're designed.

So, if you don't have the type of personality to enjoy the club, nor are you a closet bedroom rock dancer, perhaps you can try contemporary dance, where movements just reflect your current emotions. This is why dance, like music, can be used by autistic people to convey emotions that they may otherwise have a hard time expressing. It includes them in a community, which they may find very difficult to do without dance. In that, there are lessons for all of us. Dance, as a medium, can help every one of us validate, express, and share our emotions. That can be done by chair dancing in your car or office right now, or breaking into a Ginger Rogers and Fred Astaire dance with your partner on a rainy street corner.

If any of you have watched the movie *Footloose*, you know that sometimes cultures have tried to stop others from dancing. Almost every generation has felt that the next generation's dance is inappropriate. Such prohibitions often come from moral or religious beliefs that tend to criticize self-expression and individualism. When we constrict those things as a culture or society, they invariably come out in other ways. Suppressing emotions leads to anxiety, stress, depression, and can make us live a life driven by fear, which can also cause violence.

Cultures that have prohibited dance see declines in community bonding and creativity, resulting in stagnation as a people. However, dance almost always survives "underground."

The U.S. saw this in the 1920s with the Charleston and the shimmy dances that were, at the time, considered very scandalous. Those dances nowadays would be considered tame. In the end, the dances of each era reflect the constraints of society and the people's attempt to break those constraints. Invariably, that results in judgment from the generation in power at the time.

Dance often leads to societal change. In South Africa, gumboot dancing symbolized resilience during apartheid. The U.S. had prohibition-era dances like the Charleston, which I just mentioned. In more recent times, hip hop and street dancing became statements against poverty and racism. Krumping, which came from LA, expresses resilience in response to the violence suffered by minorities.

~~~~~~~~~~~~~~~

Apart from the mental health downsides of not dancing, there are numerous physical effects, as well. Physical inactivity has well-documented health risks, higher rates of obesity, cardiovascular disease, and mental health issues. Dancing regularly can eliminate all of that and is free. We can train ourselves to be attuned to dance.

The movie *August Rush* explains how the lead character, a young boy, experiences the world. He does so through the sounds that fill his everyday life—from the trash collector to the birds in the trees, to the clicking of glasses on a waiter's serving platter. He hears music and its rhythm. That is why some of the most amazing beats come from the simplest objects, like five-gallon plastic buckets and metal lids. It is not the object making the rhythm, but what we hear in our minds and how it makes our body and passions react.
~~~~~~~~~~~~~~~

You can find a reason to dance literally anywhere, from the pitter-patter of raindrops on your roof to the construction workers' sounds in your neighborhood. You just have to listen for it.

Children seem to have this gift naturally, and we lose it as we grow older, but personally, I would like to find it again. I want to hear the music and the rhythm in my everyday life. As I'm writing this, I'm riding a train to Paris, and it just occurred to me that there is a symphony of what I would normally think of as noise. Today, I'm hearing it more like a beat and rhythm of my trip. And it makes me want to nod my head in time.

~~~~~~~~~~~~~~~

I asked a friend of mine named Stella about dancing. She told me that if she isn't on stage, she's dancing in her bedroom, and that she has dance on her mind throughout the day. She explained that dance is a way to express herself and makes her feel happy.

I liked the idea she shared of dancing in her head. That means you can dance anytime, even if you can't physically get up and dance.

~~~~~~~~~~~~~~~

I used to get a little annoyed when I heard the kids making noise while I was working because I felt I needed quiet when I worked. But one day, I just realized that's wrong.

I should embrace the noise and the sounds of playing because they're having fun. What's more important than that? So, from that point on, every time I hear them playing in the pool or running up and down the stairs, it gives me joy instead of making me feel annoyed. I find that very powerful, the little changes we can make to our minds to change our world.

This is probably why, in part, people have a different affinity for different places. We like the sounds. We like the emotions that a certain place evokes. There are people who love cities. I love being by a stream and hearing the birds. My husband likes the crashing of the ocean waves. In those sounds, we feel resonance that matches our lives, and it makes us feel connected and alive.

That is dance. It is the dance of sounds that makes our souls happy.

When we're happy, we move differently from when we're sad. You know the look when someone is sad—the hunched over shoulders, the head down, the shuffling... When we're happy, there is a spring to our footsteps and a purpose to our walk. Our arms swing more, and our body moves. That is a type of dance. It is the dance we feel from the bottom of our feet to the top of our heads.

In fact, the way we hold our bodies can affect our emotions. Try something for me if it's safe: Put your head down. Hunch your shoulders and wrap your arms around yourself. What does that feel like?

OK, next, do a little tap dance. Smile. Hold your head up and spin in a circle. How does that feel?

According to Psychology Today, expressing our emotions through movement is called "the embodiment of emotions." There is a whole field of study on this. That is exactly what dance does for us. We can create a mood of our choice through the dance that we choose. Imagine being able to choose how you feel by the music and dance you will do. Well, you don't have to imagine it because you can do it almost anytime and anywhere we wish.

We have the ultimate mood changer at our fingertips that does not require illicit drugs, alcohol, or any bad side effects attached to it (well, except for maybe a little sweat). So let's just start dancing, and if someone is watching, or the whole world, maybe they will join in.

Fifteen Seconds to Change Your World

How about you? For the next fifteen seconds, can you shut your ears to the normal sounds around you and listen with the ears of a child? Can you find a beat, a tune, or a rhythm where you are right now? Let's try it and see what you hear.

My Fifteen Seconds

First of all, it's a windy day today, so I hear the wind brushing against everything outside. Earlier, my daughter and her friend were playing in the pool outside my window, so I could hear them playing, things like happy screams and jumping into the water. Later, I heard them going up the stairs with their happy footsteps.

~~~~~~~~~~~~~~~~

Humans have an amazing gift that we don't talk about much. We
~~~~~~~~~~~~~~~~

have the ability to create. I'm not just talking about creating little humans. We can create all kinds of things from abstract ideas to literal rockets that go to Mars.

But creating things is not just for fun. It does things to us and for us. That is what we'll discuss in our next chapter together.

Citations and references for this chapter are located at the end of the book.

You Are a Creator

"Creator." The word itself is magical. It conjures up the image of someone who makes something from nothing. When I spoke that word, perhaps you saw an image of a godlike being, or the science fiction personification of one. Perhaps you saw a master baker, an architect, or a builder. Maybe you pictured a child building with Legos.

Do you remember seeing something that really struck you? A painting? A model train or a beautiful pastry? A dance? Or, yes, even a Lego construct? You might have asked, "Who made this?" Perhaps you received that special reply, "I made it." It is most often said not with a sense of arrogance or superiority, but a sense of pride.

When a person utters those words, don't they seem to stand a bit taller? Their voice is a little stronger. They are more attached and present. To make something, especially from nothing, is one of the most wonderful feelings of accomplishment that humans can ever attain, and we learn that feeling from a very young age.

This feeling of pride and satisfaction from creating something is unique to humans, although other creatures do make things. Crows are known to make tools. Beavers make dams. Ants make ant hills with miles of corridors and rooms. Bees make hives. Birds make music. They all do this as a part of their innate instinct. It is not a mental decision for them to create for the sake of creating. Only humans do that.

About a year ago, at a party, I was introduced to some other musicians. Right before I was introduced to a certain producer, the person with me whispered in my ear, "He's a creator." When I heard that word used, I wasn't even sure what it meant in the context of a musician, but I knew it was the highest compliment.

Later, I listened to that person's music, and I had to agree that the best term I could think of for what I heard was "creator." I had never experienced anything like their music. Right now, I'm privileged to have that producer working with me on the most unique song I've ever written for my 2025 The Smile Project. It's called "Looking for a Thread." The GRAMMY®-winning producer I'm talking about is Kitt Wakeley, who is a wonderful human being.

"Looking for a Thread"

Experience this unique song I wrote, produced with the help of Kitt Wakeley, by scanning the QR code below.

In talking with many, many musicians, and for the sake of this discussion today, I'm referring to people who write original compositions. I discovered that almost all of them believe in a God or a higher power. The reason is simple: These musicians cannot explain how they have the gift that they do. They know, as I do, that they did not create this gift. It was given to us and is beyond our explanation.

Musicians, like artists, architects, poets, and so many others, create something that has never existed before. We do it because we see it or feel it, like unseen hands or thoughts guiding us. That feeling is something I will never grow tired of, and it constantly amazes and surprises me. I cannot take credit for it. I know someone gave me that gift. The reason I bring this up is that I am convinced only a Creator would feel compelled to create another being who can create.

Not only does it take an immense amount of trust to give creatures the ability to create other things from nothing, but it is also an awesome expression of love. Creating something makes you feel special, full, and wonderful. When we create something, it not only feels special to us, but it also makes others appreciate it. That is why bakers bake, and chefs cook. It is why architects design and choreographers create dances, and why people spend countless hours writing inspirational quotes for greeting cards, simply so that others can be moved and wowed.

I've talked about awe before, but this is a little different. Awe is about that special feeling when time slows down, and you feel as if you are observing something as a privileged guest—a sunset, the Aurora Borealis, or the birth of a child. That is awe. This time, I'm referring to our response to seeing something that was created out of nothing. Perhaps we have seen a thousand cakes and thousands of houses, but each is a unique creation, and they can surprise and awe. How many bakery windows have you walked by and marveled or drooled at the offerings?

You may be thinking to yourself right now that you are not gifted, that you can't make anything, but I guarantee you're wrong. I'm going to show you that not only can you create something, but you can do it in fifteen seconds or less. In doing so, you will bring joy to your day and a smile to your face, and likely to someone else's.

~~~~~~~~~~~~~~~

Creating things makes us happy. When we're happy, our happiness spreads. The creative process, which we learn as children, is incredibly healing and fulfilling. We learn about this when we draw a picture, and Mom or Dad reacts, even if it is a badly drawn horse with three legs and one ear. Or that amazing reaction we got when we picked a bouquet of weeds because we thought dandelions were beautiful? (They are, by the way). We get that positive feedback, so we keep doing it.

How many chefs do you think became chefs at thirty-five years old? More likely, they started cooking very young and got that wondrous response, "This is delicious!" to their first mud pie. That simple statement may have set in stone that young boy's or girl's career path.

I recently interviewed my amazing French singer from my "Could You Lend Me A Smile?" project. Her name is Katleen, and she is wonderful. I asked her why she sang. Without hesitation, she said
~~~~~~~~~~~~~~~

that when she was thirteen, she sang "The Prayer" in front of a crowd. People cried and praised her. That moment set her life's purpose in motion.

Now, some of you quick thinkers may be saying to yourself, "But she didn't create that song. It was written by someone else." You would, of course, be correct. But when Katleen sang that song, she created emotions in another person, and she wanted to experience that moment over and over again for the rest of her life.

I learned something as I wrote this chapter: I started out thinking that making physical things could change our world, and it does. They do in a very literal way. We're going to imitate some of those ideas later. But it occurred to me that humans have an additional, very special ability.

What we create does not have to be physical. Humans can create feelings and emotions in other people. We can also create thoughts and motivations, to some extent. We can inspire and set examples. Those are all types of creation. Many times, we do it without thinking about it.

"Make Me Smile"

What I am suggesting today, however, is that we do it more purposefully. That was my intent when I wrote the theme song to my podcast, *"Make Me Smile,"* I wanted to create an inviting room where you and I could spend time away from our stressful world and just share a few moments together to laugh, listen, and smile. I'd like to share a little clip of that song right now, as it has a lot to say on this subject.

After a long, long day, I would love someone to take my hand, give me a comfy chair to snuggle up in, and make me laugh or smile. We do not have to be gifted to do that for someone. We can all take turns being that extra bit of strength and "oomph" we need on those long, long days.

For instance, a child may be struggling with math homework. At that moment, we have the ability to create an emotion, motivation, or inspiration. Think of how the following sentences could do that: "You are just not good at math. You should give up." Discouragement, right?

"I really struggled with math too when I was your age." That's encouragement and support.

"Did you know that math can help you make rockets, cookies, or design clothes?" Motivation.

"If you continue to learn math, you could be the next Albert Einstein!" Inspiration.

How about another example? Think of a coach of a basketball team, and they're down eight points with seven seconds left to play. "Let's give up. We can't win this." How would the team react? The team will just give up. The comments create defeatism.

"Did you know Reggie Miller scored eight points in six seconds?" That creates belief. It's possible.

"Remember, this game is supposed to be fun. Let's go out and have fun." That creates positivity.

"The owner just texted me and said that if we win this, you all get one-million-dollar bonuses." Creativity and motivation.

Are you starting to see how we can all be creators? Not just by the things we do, but by the things we say. After all, we create the world we live in, right? If we all throw trash out of the window, we live in a garbage dump. If we throw out verbal garbage, we live in a verbal garbage dump. If we all smile at each other, we live in a happier world. I truly believe that fifteen seconds can change our world. Every single one of those sentences that I just read took less than fifteen seconds. Every one of those sentences would have affected the world for that child or that team.

There has been a lot written about the thirty-six questions that can make you fall in love. This is a series of questions that researchers have stated can make two people fall in love if they ask each other the questions. Whether or not that is true, we do know that what we say and how we act can create feelings in other people. When someone is rude to you, how do you feel? Think about the last time that happened and what that felt like. Did you feel your face flush? That metaphorical punch in the gut. The breath you held.

While it's true that we only feel what we allow ourselves to feel, other people do affect us. On the contrary, imagine someone gives you an enormous smile followed by a compliment like, "You are just amazing. I love your thoughtfulness. I really love being your friend." How do those words make you feel?

The words and tone we use, along with our facial and body expressions, can create emotions and feelings. That should give us pause. This is especially true for those of us who directly impact others, like parents, employers, positions of authority, or those with a bigger voice, like the media.

I think that parents have the biggest responsibility. After all, we are raising, teaching, and setting the example for the next generation of humans. Parents have the privilege of teaching their children that creating and making things, tangible and intangible, is important.

This is even more crucial in this time of technology. Children don't have to use their imagination anymore. The technology will do it all for them, but just because it can does not mean it's beneficial. In fact, it has been shown repeatedly to be detrimental. Children who create things with their hands and imagination, whether it is from a pile of sticks or rocks or an imaginary world in their bedroom or backyard, are calmer, able to control their emotions better, and they learn patience and creativity.

Playing with our kids, starting with "peekaboo" when they're a few days old, teaches them object permanence and the concept of a 3D world. Playing puzzles and games with them helps them prioritize, challenge themselves, control their emotions, and plan. As they get older, playing sports or doing projects with them builds confidence, helps them understand the potential of their bodies, and hones their coordination, strength, and motor skills. All of these things create a connection and a bond crucial to becoming a well-balanced adult.

That well-balanced adult will affect many others in their lifetime. As parents, we have the privilege of teaching our children that what they create with their hands and with their words affects others and can be either a powerful gift or a powerful weapon.

Teachers also have that special ability to create. If you're like me, you remember that one teacher who made an impact on you. I just watched a French movie called *The Choir*. It is about a teacher who went to work at an orphanage for difficult boys. He used choir music to bring them together and give them hope. He did that by making them believe they had something of value in themselves and each other.

A similar movie in the U.S. is *Mr. Holland's Opus,* where a music teacher inspires children to see their potential through the power of music.

These are not accidental outcomes. Those teachers purposefully sought to create good in human beings, and they did it both with physical things—music—and intangible things like love and confidence.

Parents and teachers help us create the most important thing we will make in our lives—ourselves. *Parents and teachers help us create ourselves.* That sentence struck me as I wrote it because it reminds me that my most important job, and honestly, the best thing I will ever do, is to raise my daughter to be a good human being. I can do that by helping her create the best person she can be. That is a huge responsibility, but also a beautiful one. I love it, and also struggle with it. I am more determined than ever to help create that human instead of relinquishing that privilege to an electronic device.

~~~~~~~~~~~~~~~~

Comedians are one of the most interesting types of creators. Their sole goal is to make people laugh. Laughing makes people happy, so comedians are happy mediums. They take our crazy lives and turn them into something we can laugh about. If they're really good, they can even make us cry and feel happy at the same time. What a crazy gift! But that life goal of creating happiness and laughter is one of the highest pursuits we can have.

If you ask any comedian why they do it, they'll likely say it's to create a moment of comic relief in a difficult world. That relief also bonds us as a community. When we laugh together, we're less likely to fight with each other. That's a good thing.

~~~~~~~~~~~~~~

I spent several days touring museums in Europe. They were packed with people from all over the world. Why were we all there? To see amazing art, sculptures, and ideas from people who, for the most part, had long passed away.

Decades, centuries, or even thousands of years later, those works of art evoke feelings and emotions in us, and that is the artist's or sculptor's purpose. They create a piece of art that creates an emotion.

It's not always the same emotion, either. There is definitely awe in some. Others make you laugh. Some make you sad.

A particular artist in the Musée Rodin in Paris made me a little scared. He painted pictures of people's memories, ghost-like figures that were not menacing or fearful, just people long gone who used to be in that place where he painted them. At least, that is what I felt when I saw his art.

Creative artists, including contemporary dancers, can create emotions that surprise us; they intentionally do it. Why? It connects us. It draws us into a world where we are at our most basic and the same. We fear. We laugh. We're sad. We're determined. We're strong, and we are weak. We are human.

So, as we, including myself, sit here and think, "I'm no Michael Angelo or van Gogh. I'm not Nate Bargatze or Fred Astaire. I can't create emotions as they do." I'm going to say I have to disagree.

Today, we can make it a point to create one hundred, two hundred, or even more smiles by simply smiling at people. Those smiles don't exist right now. If you want to make a couple of hundred people smile and laugh at one time, you can do that by simply acting silly in a crowded place. Try skipping and holding hands with a friend.

Whether we are a comedian, a parent, a teacher, a cook, a janitor, or a domestic engineer, we should never stop creating. Never stop making things with our hands. Never stop creating imagination and daydreams in ourselves and our children. Never stop creating confidence and happiness in others.

We were given the gift of being creators, so let's use that to create, not to tear down. Let's create communities instead of disparity and happiness instead of sadness. Let's create the world we want to live in, a world where we all create smiles every day.

~~~~~~~~~~~~~~~~

We have talked a lot about so many things we can create, but now for the fun part. I mentioned in the beginning that some of you think you cannot create anything, but that is not true, both in a physical sense and an impactful sense. This time, let's do a couple of fifteen-second exercises. You can pick one or both, but as we do these fifteen-second actions, let's notice how it makes us feel. Contemplate what we will do, contemplate while we're doing it, and then after we're finished with the action.

Fifteen Seconds to Change Your World

The first one is to create a physical thing. If you're at home, you can grab a piece of paper, a pen, a paperclip, a stack of crackers, forks, and spoons, and build something. Draw something. Make something. If you're at a loss, pretend you're five years old, and you are bored out of your brain, and imagine something.

If you're driving, you can create a new dance with your fingers, arm, head, or whole body, or thump out a rhythm on your steering wheel with your hands.

My Fifteen Seconds
~~~~~~~~~~~~~~~~

I took a piece of Kleenex and two pieces of tape and made a kind of ball. I was hoping it would bounce better, but it doesn't really. However, if I hit it with my hand, it actually bounces almost like a badminton birdie. It made me feel very proud. I'm not sure if I'm strange, but every time I make something weird, I'm just so proud of myself. I like to share those ideas with my daughter. Sometimes it annoys her. Sometimes she loves it. Either way, it makes me very happy. What did you do?

Fifteen Seconds to Change Your World

This exercise is not as easy, but it's more impactful to others. Think about a person that you care about. If you're a boss, think about an employee you see potential in. Think of a parent or one of your children. Got them in mind?

Now, think about a feeling you would like them to experience today. It could be feeling happy, loved, proud, confident... Whatever feeling you want to create in that person. Got it?

Now we want to do something to create that feeling. Normally, I would say not to use technology to do an action, but for this one, I think it is OK. Make a phone call, send a text, maybe with emojis, or better yet, have a face-to-face interaction. Try to create that feeling in the other person.

For instance, if you want them to feel loved, you could tell them why you love them. If you want to give them confidence, compliment them on something they recently did. If you want them to be happy, send them a silly emoji, meme, or give them a goofy smile.

Remember, there are three phases here: how you're feeling while thinking about what you are going to do, how you feel while doing it, and how you feel *after* doing it.

My Fifteen Seconds

I thought of my mom and wanted to create a feeling of being loved and accepted. So, I told her, "Mom, I appreciate everything you do for my family and me. However, I love you the same, even if you don't do anything for us."

She had this look that I rarely see on her face, either with me or with others. She is a people pleaser and works to earn acceptance wherever she goes. I shocked her by saying that. I think what I told her is also something that she's wanted to hear for a long time. I'm glad I did it, and it made me very happy.

I wanted us to pay attention to how we felt when we were planning the action because it made us happy. Likewise, we will do those actions more often by remembering how we feel while we're doing them and how we feel afterward. It depends on the response, but when you get that positive response, remembering that you made someone's day will help you want to do it again.

Citations and references for this chapter are located at the end of the book.

Unfailing Love

I was writing songs for my first album, *The Songs from the Living Room*. A very well-known producer surprised me and told me he wanted a song that made him cry. I love writing emotional songs, so I wrote him what I thought was a real tear-jerker and let him listen to it. He didn't cry.

He asked me to write him another one, then another. Finally, I asked him what subject or emotion would make him cry, and he described his touching relationship with his mom. I went home and wrote a song called "Love Them Away."

"Love Them Away"

When I played him this song, he got very emotional and said, "That's it!" The song is about acceptance. The deep-down need all of us have to be loved for who we truly are, no matter what happens.

There was a particular line that seemed to affect him the most. It goes, "No fear. Show who you are to me. I'll count all your tears, your nightmares, and fears and love them away." Some people would call this kind of love unconditional love, but that is not really what I meant.

In my chapter entitled, "Why Do We Love?" I talked a lot about the different kinds of love. One of those kinds of love is the kind that the Greeks referred to as "agape." It is a principled love often described as being unconditional.

But unconditional love would include being able to love someone or something despite them doing horrible things or being a horrible person. Unconditional love literally would mean loving even someone who could find joy in hurting or killing other people. That is not what the Greeks had in mind with "agape."

"Agape" was a love that could be shown to all people and beings, whether they were known to a person or not. In other words, you can show "agape" to someone you've never met and might never meet again by simply smiling at them or being kind just because you can. You could send a gift to a total stranger, and that may also count as showing "agape" love.

When the term is used in the Bible, it refers to God giving rain and produce to everyone, not just believers. However, that was not what I was trying to convey in "Love Them Away."

I normally have a very specific story when I write a song, but in this case, I had two. In the first one, I saw a young child scared and crying because they're afraid to tell their parent what they have done. The parent responds, "Have no fear. You can show who you really are to me, and I promise that I will love away all your fears." That is something I never experienced as a child, but a scene that I often daydreamed might happen one day. Sadly, with my parents, it never did, but that is why I was able to write it from a child's point of view.

The second story is a little more complex, something I think many of us have done as adults. I often ended up in relationships where I showed only the best side of myself. I could have been with a person for months or even years, but I had always been afraid to show everything about myself. It's scary to do that. You fear the other person might be disgusted or not love you anymore. It's been said, "Falling in love is terrifying." It certainly can be, especially if you are unsure of why the other person loves you.

I imagined a scene where a person was in love and desperately wanted to feel completely safe and secure. They needed to feel calm without fear of losing the other person. There were things they were terrified to talk about, like things in their past or desires and thoughts they had. That is when I imagined this amazing partner telling the one in fear, "If you don't have the words, I'll understand. Your heart will always be safe in my hands. It will. There's nothing you could do to make me walk away. I promise you I'm here to stay."

I was well into my thirties when I experienced this. I had a partner who not only said those words to me but truly felt them. Everyone wants to have this feeling. It is the most freeing and calming emotion that we can experience. It is love, but it's a specific kind, and I struggled for weeks to describe it in words.

When I researched this idea or thought, I always came back to unconditional love. But as I mentioned, that is not accurate because I could not love a person no matter what they did or who they were. If they were a psychotic killer, I could not love them, but I know my husband is not one. The fact that I know who he truly is and he knows who I truly am, flaws and all, results in a particular kind of love.

I find it remarkable that we do not have a common expression that clearly identifies this feeling—knowing someone so well that we have no doubt as to who they are, and they do likewise for us, providing that perfect bubble of emotional safety. It is at that point we can love them, and this is the word I was struggling for: "unfailingly." We truly know someone when they're free to express their secret feelings, strengths, desires, dislikes, the way they need to be held, and when they need to be let go. We know 100 percent in our hearts and minds that we know them completely through and through. Then we can have unfailing love, a love that never fails. That is the love that I wrote about in "Love Them Away."

Why do we so badly want the feeling of being completely accepted and free to be who we truly are? To answer that question, I got to thinking about the special love between a child and a parent.

To clarify, I didn't feel that kind of love very much when I was a child, but every child knows what it should feel like. So, when it is not there, we still know we want it. That relationship between a child and a parent is a dependent one. The child is physically dependent on the parents for things like food, shelter, and protection, but it is also emotionally dependent. The child needs to feel safe and loved to grow in a healthy way. The dependence creates a bond, an extremely strong one that is meant to last a lifetime. We often call children "mama's boys" or "daddy's girls" for a reason.

That special bond between a parent and a child is often unfailing. It is as permanent a bond as we can experience in this world.

Dependence can create a situation where the connection between two people (or between a person and a thing) causes emotional reliance. That reliance can turn into love. For instance, a pet that is reliant on a person or even a plant that we take care of. It creates a bond of love.

I experienced this on a family vacation in Hawaii. On a beach, there was a pigeon that was all by itself, and it looked hurt. I went over to it and started feeding it corn chips. Within a few minutes, I could petit, and it cooed when it wanted more food. It also started acting better and being more active, which made me feel better. By the time I left an hour later, I was attached to that bird to the point where I thought about it all week. I know it was a dependent relationship, but it felt like a real bond.

In that, there is some insight. To create unfailing love, you must be dependent on each other. On the other hand, that dependence must not be abused. Otherwise, it does not grow into a healthy love.

Two people who have unfailing love between them are always dependent on each other. Oftentimes, highly independent people, like I was, end up sabotaging themselves in the relationships that we actually deserve because we refuse to become dependent on anyone. While that could include physical or material dependence, it doesn't have to.

In fact, those dependencies may make it harder to feel unfailing love because of the power dynamic that has to be dealt with, complicating matters and even injecting doubt and resentment into the relationship. I'm not saying that type of relationship cannot have unfailing love, but it would be more difficult and requires great awareness from the partners.

In contrast, two highly independent and successful people can choose to be dependent on each other and create this unfailing love bond. It is not that they don't value their independence, but that they see the tremendous value, comfort, and safety in that person, so they choose to be vulnerable and dependent on someone else. They want a partner in life to know who they truly are, not just the face they put on in business, social situations, or online. That desire to be loved for who we truly and completely are is universal.

As mentioned, a dependency may be physical and material, but unfailing love must include emotional and mental dependency. It is a feeling more than a specific action. It is a feeling of peace and calmness without pretense. It is the comfort we find when we're allowed to be completely ourselves, but with the added love of another person. It feels like home.

For these reasons, unfailing love is a noun, not a verb. "I love you" is a verb. "Unfailing love," however, is a noun. While we can show love by our actions, unfailing love is how we feel about the other person. From that, we learn that unfailing love requires more than actions. When you think of the greatest acts of love—for instance, sacrificing our lives for someone—those actions would never happen if we didn't first have an extreme feeling of love towards the other person. That feeling creates the ability to make such a sacrifice.

So, if we want to both feel and provide unfailing love for another person, it starts with how we feel. As is often the case, how we feel about ourselves has a huge impact on how we feel about another person. A person who doesn't love themselves will have a very difficult time showing and feeling love to someone else, because if we judge ourselves harshly, we tend to impose that judgment on others.

In other words, if we have a bad thought, then we condemn ourselves for it. What is the likelihood of us sharing that bad thought with someone else? If, by chance, our partner admits to the same bad thought, we have to judge them as we have judged ourselves. Once we show that we are going to judge someone else, what is the likelihood that they'll share their true feelings and thoughts with us?

On the other hand, if we accept that we have bad thoughts periodically, but this does not make us a bad person, then when someone else shares their bad thoughts with us, we will not be judgmental. That creates the possibility of emotional dependency. In the words of "Love Them Away," "I'm not here for only a day or a year. We will be, you and me, until forever."

Unfailing love is that bond of emotional dependency created in a non-judgmental relationship. That doesn't mean we accept bad behavior or even wrong thoughts, but we accept that everyone has bad behaviors and wrong thoughts. We accept that it is OK because we know those wrong thoughts do not define them or us.

Unfailing love often survives the death of one of the partners because the peace that comes from having been in an unfailing love relationship can provide a measure of emotional sustenance to us, even if we lose that partner to death. After all, knowing that someone truly understood every part of us and still loved us unfailingly is a powerful affirmation.

Judgmental people find it very difficult, if not impossible, to find unfailing love because they are always judging themselves. Thus, they are judging others, and that, by definition, does not provide an emotionally safe relationship.

As with almost all of the principles we talk about in *Make Me Smile*, it starts with ourselves. If you come from a culture like mine, learning to be non-judgmental can feel contrary to our entire upbringing. Many cultures carry guilt and judgment almost as a flag of pride. They like to criticize, point out flaws, and demean anything less than perfection. They think it is motivational.

If we come from one of those cultures, we have to first fight that inclination to imitate our own inclination and ancestry. That is not easy, but think of how freeing that would feel to be rid of that unrelenting pressure. I can say from personal experience, it is a relief, not unlike the removal of my seven-inch liver tumor. It is that significant and wonderful.

This doesn't mean that unfailing love does not involve action. Our action, or inaction, often lays the basis for creating a bond with another. When a highly stressed, sleep-deprived new mother confesses feeling that she sometimes wants to leave her child, we can react with understanding, not judgment. When a teenager talks about not caring about anything or anyone or wanting to experiment with drugs, we can listen with understanding of the pressures of being a young person in this hypercritical world.

Sometimes, no reaction is the best thing. Oftentimes, the people expressing those thoughts are in a highly vulnerable place, and they are expressing thoughts, not imminent action. We can react as we would like someone else to if it were us: with understanding, patience, and a listening ear. When we do that, we invite dependency and form an emotional bond.

Given this understanding, it's not surprising that sometimes the most celebrated artists are those who show the world their deepest, darkest fears. In books, songs, and art, mankind's history is replete with tortured souls, fighting wrong thoughts and oftentimes failing. It is those very feelings that attract us, and they also tell on us.

If we are outwardly or inwardly critical of those people who expose their fears to the world, then what is the likelihood that we will be able to share our fears with anyone? Revealing my deepest fears and insecurities to you has shown me this is true. The more songwriting I do, the more vulnerable I am, the stronger I become, and the freer I am. I am always trying to live a life as close to my true self as possible, as it just feels right. I think I now understand what the saying means to "be comfortable in your own skin."

I love that feeling of finally fitting into my own skin. There is a Chinese song, "The Love Song on the Radio." It has beautiful lyrics about turning off the moonlight because it shines too brightly on the love between us, and our love can't handle the scrutiny. The neon signs tell the story of our love, but it's all a fairytale because we haven't found a way to really show ourselves to each other.

It tells the pain of not finding unfailing love. We want the fairytale ending, but we're too afraid of showing who we really are. We want someone to love away our fears, but we are too scared that our fears will scare everyone away. That is just not true. Finding someone worthy and able to receive and give unfailing love is worth everything in the world because without that feeling, we feel as if we're living in someone else's world instead of one we belong in.

~~~~~~~~~~~~~~~

I watched a show called *Younger* on Netflix, and a particular line really struck me. One of the characters was attempting to help someone understand why they kept getting into doomed relationships and said to them, "We often accept the love we think we deserve" (the character was evidently quoting Stephen Chbosky).

That really hit me as true. In life, we can easily settle on a relationship without unfailing love because deep down, we feel we do not deserve it. We feel we do not deserve to be loved completely and wholly without fear of betrayal or abandonment. We think that, because we are inherently flawed and imperfect, it's just not something we have earned. That is how I felt for most of my life, but even saying those words feels wrong because every person deserves to be loved unfailingly, and that includes you and me.

In a previous chapter, I asked you to finish the sentence "I am..." I
~~~~~~~~~~~~~~~

had some wonderful responses to that challenge, but I'd like to delve more into the question, "Who am I?"

The question has to do with finding our place in this world, where we belong, and our innate desire to discover the answer to this most basic of questions. Experiencing unfailing love would allow us to find out who we really are. Without it, we may always wonder who that is.

Fifteen Seconds to Change Your World

Finding unfailing love is a process; it has to start somewhere. Take a baby step today and tell someone something about yourself that you have never told them before. That someone could be a child, a parent, or a friend, but it must be someone you see as having the potential for an unfailing love relationship.

If you just can't find someone to tell that tidbit about, tell yourself out loud. Speak the words or text them to yourself. Obviously, with this exercise, use wisdom to decide what to share and with whom.

This is the first step, so it doesn't have to be a huge secret. It could be that you secretly love the color purple or that you wish you could live on a farm. Just something meaningful and true that just might lead to a wonderful conversation and a bond.

My Fifteen Seconds

My secret is that I'm afraid of reading comments because I don't believe my newly built, still fragile confidence can survive any bad comments. It doesn't mean that I don't read them. I ask my husband to screen them for me.

Thankfully, I've been getting nothing but encouraging and heartwarming comments. Thank you all for that.

<center>~~~~~~~~~~~~~~~</center>

Unfailing love isn't loud or flashy most of the time. It isn't a perfect fairytale or riding off into the sunset of a Hollywood ending. It shows up in quiet ways and in everyday, ordinary moments—even messy ones. It can mean making coffee for someone when you're mad at them, sitting in silence when words won't fix it, or driving across town just because they need you. It can even mean having an argument, then hugging it out. Unfailing love is, after all, about learning to accept our own imperfections and to see past the imperfections of others. By doing so, we just may find someone who will sit with us for a lifetime... and longer.

<center>~~~~~~~~~~~~~~~</center>

I hope you enjoyed spending time with me on this adaptation of my *Make Me Smile With Miist* podcast.

I would love it if you joined me for the next twenty-four episodes in Volume II. Below you will find a preview of the subjects I talk about there. You can also listen to all these episodes now on any streaming platform. This QR code will take you directly to the podcast page on my website.

#25. Who Am I?

#26. Great Expectations

#27. The Story in Our Ears

#28. Please Don't Bother Me. I'm Dreaming.

#29. Why Should I be Patient?

#30. Revenge. Who Pays?

#31. Do We Live for the Past, the Future, or Today?

#32. Artificial What?

#33. What's in a Name?

#34. Why Be Different?

#35. Inspiring Talk

#36. Selfish or Generous. Which?

#37. Stop Comparing

#38. Take it Slow

#39. Three Days To Say Goodbye

#40. Life is About Choices. Right?

#41. Regret

#42. Is Cleanliness Really Next to Godliness?

#43. Shame on Me

#44. The Brian's

#45. Challenge Me

#46. Let's Get Bored

#47. It Shouldn't Be That Easy

#48. Be Authentic

Sources

1958 Pianist Glenn Gould Program Piano Concert Bach Bartók Mozart. ValueYourMusic, 2017. https://www.valueyourmusic.com/items/272838602926-1958-pianist-glenn-gould-program-piano-concert-bach-bartok-mozart-ipo-israel-vr.

Alhawatmeh, Haneen, Rawan Albataineh, and Shorouq Abuhammad. "Differential Effects of Guided Imagery and Progressive Muscle Relaxation on Physical and Emotional Symptoms in Nursing Students Taking Initial Clinical Training: A Randomized Clinical Trial." Heliyon 8, no. 10 (2022): e11147. https://doi.org/10.1016/j.heliyon.2022.e11147.

Anticevic, Aleksandar, Michael W. Cole, Jonathan D. Murray, Philip R. Corlett, Xiao-Jing Wang, and John H. Krystal. "The Role of Default Network Deactivation in Cognition and Disease." Trends in Cognitive Sciences 16, no. 12 (2012): 584–92. https://doi.org/10.1016/j.tics.2012.10.008.

Anwar, Yasmin. "Creating Love in the Lab: The 36 Questions That Spark Intimacy." University of California News, February 14, 2015. https://www.universityofcalifornia.edu/news/creating-love-lab-36-questions-spark-intimacy.

Association for Psychological Science. "Ability to Identify Genuine Laughter Transcends Culture." Association for Psychological Science, 2026. https://www.psychologicalscience.org/news/releases/ability-to-identify-genuine-laughter-transcends-culture.html.

Ate Bijlsma, Azar, Azar Omrani, Martijn Spoelder, Jeroen P. H. Verharen, Lars Bauer, Cornelis Cornelis, René van Dorland, Louk Beleke de Zwart, and Corette J. Wierenga. "Social Play Behavior Is Critical for the Development of Prefrontal Inhibitory Synapses and Cognitive Flexibility in Rats." Journal of Neuroscience 42, no. 46 (2022): 8716–28. https://doi.org/10.1523/JNEUROSCI.0524-22.2022.

Bai, Y., J. Ocampo, G. Jin, S. Chen, Veronica Benet-Martínez, M. Monroy, C. Anderson, and Dacher Keltner. "Awe, Daily Stress, and Elevated Life Satisfaction." Journal of Personality and Social Psychology 120, no. 4 (2021): 837–60. https://doi.org/10.1037/pspa0000267.

Banerjee, Pooja. "Salvador Dalí's Surrealist Homage to Science." Down to Earth, February 15, 2025. https://www.downtoearth.org.in/science-technology/salvadore-dalis-surrealist-homage-to-science.

Bergström, Annika, Peter Okong, and Anna-Berit Ransjö-Arvidson. "Immediate Maternal Thermal Response to Skin-to-Skin Care of Newborns." Acta Paediatrica 96, no. 5 (2007): 655–58. https://doi.org/10.1111/j.1651-2227.2007.00280.x.

Blackburn, Lauren. "The Importance of Touch." Boundless, January 24, 2024. https://www.boundless.org/blog/the-importance-of-touch/.

Brown, Stuart L., and Christopher C. Vaughan. Play: How It Shapes the Brain, Opens the Imagination, and Invigorates the Soul. New York: Avery, 2009.

Buchowski, Michael S., Katherine M. Majchrzak, Kristina

Blomquist, Kong Y. Chen, David W. Byrne, and Jan-A. Bachorowski. "Energy Expenditure of Genuine Laughter." International Journal of Obesity 31, no. 1 (2006): 131–37. https://doi.org/10.1038/sj.ijo.0803353.

Calaprice, Alice. The Expanded Quotable Einstein. Princeton, NJ: Princeton University Press, 2000.

Cedeno, Rolando, and Tania J. Torrico. "Adlerian Therapy." In StatPearls. Treasure Island, FL: StatPearls Publishing, 2024. https://www.ncbi.nlm.nih.gov/books/NBK599518/.

Chapman, Gary D. The 5 Love Languages. Chicago: Northfield Publishing, 2014.

Cheng, Ting, and Alessandra Cataldo. "Touch and Other Somatosensory Senses." In Neuroscience of Touch. Cambridge, MA: MIT Press, 2022. https://www.ncbi.nlm.nih.gov/books/NBK583711.

Child's Play in Action. "14 Reasons You Should Play Hide and Seek Right Now." February 5, 2017. https://www.childsplayinaction.com/14-reasons-to-play-hide-and-seek/.

Chilton, Martin. "Deconstructing the Love Song: How and Why Love Songs Work." UDiscover Music, February 14, 2025. https://www.udiscovermusic.com/in-depth-features/deconstructing-the-love-song-how-they-work/.

Davis, Julie L. "Why Do We Laugh?" WebMD, n.d. https://www.webmd.com/men/features/why-do-we-laugh.

Dawson, Abigail. "The Awe-Seeker's Guide to Travel." John Templeton Foundation, December 11, 2025. https://www.templeton.org/news/the-awe-seekers-guide-to-travel.

Day, Lisa. The Power of Touch. London: Baby Sensory, 2008. https://www.babysensory.com/content/S637475378891512938/The%20Power%20of%20Touch.pdf.

Del Pozo, Javier. "Qigong for Restoration of Cognitive Function." Psychology Today, 2024. https://www.psychologytoday.com/us/blog/being-awake-better/202403/qigong-for-restoration-of-cognitive-function.

Dimitrije Curcic. "Romance Novel Sales Statistics." WordsRated, October 9, 2022. https://wordsrated.com/romance-novel-sales-statistics/.

Dobrova-Krol, Nataliya A., Marinus H. van IJzendoorn, Marian J. Bakermans-Kranenburg,

Cécile Cyr, and Femmie Juffer. "Physical Growth Delays and Stress Dysregulation in Stunted and Non-Stunted Ukrainian Institution-Reared Children." Infant Behavior and Development 31, no. 3 (2008): 539–53. https://doi.org/10.1016/j.infbeh.2008.04.001.

Do Elephants Dance? "The Truth About Their Rhythmic Movements." Biology Insights, January 7, 2026. https://biologyinsights.com/do-elephants-dance-the-truth-about-their-rhythmic-movements.

Dunbar, Robin I. M., Robin Baron, Anna Frangou, Eiluned Pearce, Edwin J. C. van Leeuwen, Jennifer Stow, Guy Partridge, Ian MacDonald, Vasilis Barra, and Mark van Vugt. "Social Laughter Is Correlated with an Elevated Pain Threshold." Proceedings of the Royal Society B: Biological Sciences 279, no. 1731 (2011): 1161–67. https://doi.org/10.1098/rspb.2011.1373.

Editors of Science News Today. "The Hidden Language of Bees and How They Dance to Communicate." Science News Today, July 29, 2025. https://www.sciencenewstoday.org/the-hidden-language-of-bees-and-how-they-dance-to-communicate.

Epictetus. Discourses. Translated by Robin Hard. New York: Penguin Classics, 2014.

Everyday Health. "How to Laugh More Every Single Day—and Why It's So Good for You." Everyday Health, n.d. https://www.everydayhealth.com/self-care/how-to-laugh-more-every-single-day-why-its-so-good-for-you/.

Feldman, David B., and Brian W. Corn. "Hope and Cancer." Current Opinion in Psychology 49 (2022): 101506. https://doi.org/10.1016/j.copsyc.2022.101506.

Feldman, Ruth, Moran Singer, and Orna Zagoory. "Touch Attenuates Infants' Physiological Reactivity to Stress." Developmental Science 13, no. 2 (2010): 271–78. https://doi.org/10.1111/j.1467-7687.2009.00890.x.

Ferguson, Phil. "Clever Hans." Encyclopaedia Britannica, n.d. https://www.britannica.com/topic/Clever-Hans.

Field, Tiffany. "Violence and Touch Deprivation in Adolescents." Adolescence 37, no. 148 (2002): 735–49. https://pubmed.ncbi.nlm.nih.gov/12564826/.

Foxwell, Jessica, Ben Alderson-Day, Charles Fernyhough, and Anna Woods. "I've Learned I Need to Treat My Characters Like People: Varieties of Agency and Interaction in Writers' Experiences of Their Characters' Voices." Consciousness and Cognition 79 (2020): 102901. https://doi.org/10.1016/j.concog.2020.102901.

Franco, Luis S., Danielle F. Shanahan, and Richard A. Fuller. "A Review of the Benefits of Nature Experiences: More Than Meets the Eye." International Journal of Environmental Research and Public Health 14, no. 8 (2017): 864. https://doi.org/10.3390/ijerph14080864.

Galoni, Caroline. "How the Specter of Contagious Disease Changes What We Want to Eat." Kellogg Insight, November 2, 2020. https://insight.kellogg.northwestern.edu/article/contagious-disease-food-choices.

George Bernard Shaw. "Quote." LibQuotes, 2017. https://libquotes.com/george-bernard-shaw/quote/lbs3w2f.

Glass, Nathan. "Word of the Week: Backpfeifengesicht." Germany in USA, February 22, 2019. https://germanyinusa.com/2019/02/22/word-of-the-week-backpfeifengesicht/.

Goss, Taryn. "The Life-Changing Power of Awe." National Geographic Health, 2025. https://www.nationalgeographic.

com/health/article/science-of-awe-health-benefits.

Gray, John. Men Are from Mars, Women Are from Venus. New York: HarperThorsons, 1997.

Gregersen, Erik. "Martin Cooper." Encyclopaedia Britannica, 2018. https://www.britannica.com/biography/Martin-Cooper.

Greteman, Bill. "How Laughter Evolved and How It Makes Us Human." Optimist Daily, 2026. https://www.optimistdaily.com/2009/08/how-laughter-evolved-and-how-it-makes-us-human/.

Gupta, Rakesh, Tracy R. Koscik, Antoine Bechara, and Daniel Tranel. "The Amygdala and Decision-Making." Neuropsychologia 49, no. 4 (2011): 760–66. https://doi.org/10.1016/j.neuropsychologia.2010.09.029.

Hallinan, Joseph. "The Remarkable Power of Hope." Psychology Today, 2014. https://www.psychologytoday.com/us/blog/kidding-ourselves/201405/the-remarkable-power-of-hope.

Halton, Mary. "Humans Are Made to Be Touched—So What Happens When We Aren't?" TED-Ed, June 17, 2021. https://ed.ted.com/blog/2021/06/17/humans-are-made-to-be-touched-so-what-happens-when-we-arent.

Harrell, Eben. "The Power of Everyday Awe." Harvard Business Review, January 1, 2023. https://hbr.org/2023/01/the-power-of-everyday-awe.

Harlow, Harry F. "The Nature of Love." American Psychologist 13, no. 12 (1958): 673–85. https://doi.org/10.1037/h0047884.

Harlow, Harry F., and Robert R. Zimmermann. "Affectional Response in the Infant Monkey." Science 130, no. 3373 (1959): 421–32. https://doi.org/10.1126/science.130.3373.421.

Herbert, Frank. Dune. New York: Chilton Books, 1965.

Hinkley, Trina, Helen Brown, Valerie Carson, and Mitch Teychenne. "Cross-Sectional Associations of Screen Time and Outdoor Play with Social Skills in Preschool Children." PLOS ONE 13, no. 4 (2018): e0193700. https://doi.org/10.1371/journal.pone.0193700.

Howell, James. Paroimiographia; or, Proverbs, or Old Sayed-Sawes & Adages in English. London, 1659.

Human Improvement Project. "The DOCS Happiness Model." n.d. https://www.humanimprovement.org/blog/the-docs-happiness-model-dopamine-oxytocin-cortisol-serotonin.

Hynek, Jakub. "What's with All the Songs About Love?" Harvard Crimson, April 23, 2018. https://www.thecrimson.com/article/2024/4/23/why-is-there-so-much-love-in-music-thinkpiece/.

Macdonald, Fiona. "Eleven Untranslatable Words." BBC Culture, October 21, 2014. https://www.bbc.com/culture/article/20140703-eleven-untranslatable-words.

Manninen, Sanna, Liisa Tuominen, Robin I. M. Dunbar, Tuomas Karjalainen, Jussi Hirvonen, Emilia Arponen, Riitta Hari, Ilkka P.

Jääskeläinen, Mikko Sams, and Lauri Nummenmaa.

"Social Laughter Triggers Endogenous Opioid Release in Humans." Journal of Neuroscience 37, no. 25 (2017): 6125–31. https://doi.org/10.1523/JNEUROSCI.0688-16.2017.

Marano, Heidi. "Laughter: The Best Medicine." Psychology Today, 2025. https://www.psychologytoday.com/us/articles/200504/laughter-the-best-medicine.

Mayo Clinic. "Stress Relief from Laughter? It's No Joke." Mayo Clinic, September 22, 2023. https://www.mayoclinic.org/healthy-lifestyle/stress-management/in-depth/stress-relief/art-20044456.

Mayo Clinic Staff. "Use Positive Self-Talk to Protect Your Health." Mayo Clinic, 2024. https://www.mayoclinic.org/connected-care/use-positive-self-talk-to-protect-your-health/vid-20508725.

McGlone, Francis, Håkan Olausson, Jason A. Boyle, Marilyn Jones-Gotman, Catriona Dancer, Simon Guest, and Gary Essick. "Touching and Feeling: Differences in Pleasant Touch Processing between Glabrous and Hairy Skin in Humans." European Journal of Neuroscience 35, no. 11 (2012): 1782–88. https://doi.org/10.1111/j.1460-9568.2012.08092.x.

Mehrabian, Albert. Silent Messages. Belmont, CA: Wadsworth, 1971.

Moyer, Melinda Wenner. "Unstructured Play Is Critical to Child Development." Scientific American, May 2016. https://www.

scientificamerican.com/article/unstructured-play-is-critical-to-child-development.

National Academies of Sciences, Engineering, and Medicine. Health Impacts of Social Isolation and Loneliness on Morbidity and Quality of Life. Washington, DC: National Academies Press, 2020. https://www.ncbi.nlm.nih.gov/books/NBK557983/.

National Institute for Play. "The Importance of Play for Adults." 2023. https://nifplay.org/play-note/adult-play/

Nicholson, Christopher. "The Humor Gap." Scientific American, October 2012. https://www.scientificamerican.com/article/the-humor-gap-2012-10-23/

Quinn, William. "LOL: Amid Uncertain Times, Consumers Take Comfort in Nostalgic Comedy Shows." Nielsen, March 19, 2021. https://www.nielsen.com/insights/2021/lol-amid-uncertain-times-consumers-take-comfort-in-nostalgic-comedy-shows/

Robson, David. "Why Do We Laugh Inappropriately?" BBC Future, 2015. https://www.bbc.com/future/article/20150320-why-do-we-laugh-inappropriately

Ross Bentley. "SAFE Is Fast." SafeIsFast.com, 2025. https://safeisfast.com/ask-a-pro/ross-bentley

Roosevelt, Franklin D. "Inaugural Address." March 4, 1933. The American Presidency Project. https://www.presidency.ucsb.edu/documents/inaugural-address-8

Sagan, Carl. Cosmos. New York: Random House, 1980.

Sebanz, Natalie, and Günther Knoblich. "Mirror Neuron." Encyclopaedia Britannica, 2019. https://www.britannica.com/science/mirror-neuron.

Schafer, Jack. "People Will Like You If You Make Them Laugh." Psychology Today, 2016. https://www.psychologytoday.com/us/blog/let-their-words-do-the-talking/201608/people-will-you-if-you-make-them-laugh.

Tan, Amy. The Joy Luck Club. New York: Penguin Books, 1989.

Thaut, Michael H., Gert C. McIntosh, and Volker Hoemberg. "Neurobiological Foundations of Neurologic Music Therapy: Rhythmic Entrainment and the Motor System." Frontiers in Psychology 5 (2015): 1185. https://doi.org/10.3389/fpsyg.2014.01185.

Tierney, Adam, and Nina Kraus. "Neural Responses to Sounds Presented On and Off the Beat of Ecologically Valid Music." Frontiers in Systems Neuroscience 7 (2013). https://doi.org/10.3389/fnsys.2013.00014.

Twain, Mark. The Adventures of Tom Sawyer. New York: American Publishing Company, 1876.

Van der Kolk, Bessel. The Body Keeps the Score: Brain, Mind, and Body in the Healing of Trauma. New York: Penguin Books, 2015.

Wetzel, Christine. "Brain Scans of Dying Man Suggest Life Flashes Before Our Eyes upon Death." Smithsonian Magazine, February 28, 2022. https://www.smithsonianmag.com/smart-news/brain-scans-suggest-life-flashes-before-our-eyes-upon-death-180979647/

Wolf, Jennifer. "Are They Friends or Not? Just a Second of Laughter Can Reveal Relationship Status, UCLA Study Finds." UCLA Newsroom, April 11, 2016. https://newsroom.ucla.edu/releases/friends-or-not-laughter-reveal-friendship-status-ucla-study

World Health Organization. "Physical Activity." June 26, 2024. https://www.who.int/westernpacific/newsroom/fact-sheets/detail/physical-activity

Zhu, Yifan, et al. "Effect of 3-Month Aerobic Dance on Hippocampal Volume and Cognition in Elderly People with Amnestic Mild Cognitive Impairment." Frontiers in Aging Neuroscience 14 (2022). https://doi.org/10.3389/fnagi.2022.